Piece by Piece

Piece by Piece

STORIES ABOUT FITTING INTO CANADA

edited by
TERESA TOTEN

PUFFIN
CANADA

PUFFIN CANADA

Published by the Penguin Group

Penguin Group (Canada), 90 Eglinton Avenue East, Suite 700, Toronto, Ontario, Canada M4P 2Y3
(a division of Pearson Canada Inc.)

Penguin Group (USA) Inc., 375 Hudson Street, New York, New York 10014, U.S.A.
Penguin Books Ltd, 80 Strand, London WC2R oRL, England
Penguin Ireland, 25 St Stephen's Green, Dublin 2, Ireland (a division of Penguin Books Ltd)
Penguin Group (Australia), 250 Camberwell Road, Camberwell, Victoria 3124, Australia
(a division of Pearson Australia Group Pty Ltd)
Penguin Books India Pvt Ltd, 11 Community Centre, Panchsheel Park, New Delhi—110 017, India
Penguin Group (NZ), 67 Apollo Drive, Rosedale, North Shore 0745, Auckland, New Zealand
(a division of Pearson New Zealand Ltd)
Penguin Books (South Africa) (Pty) Ltd, 24 Sturdee Avenue, Rosebank, Johannesburg 2196, South Africa

Penguin Books Ltd, Registered Offices: 80 Strand, London WC2R oRL, England

First published 2010

1 2 3 4 5 6 7 8 9 10 (WEB)

Introduction and selection copyright © Teresa Toten, 2010

The quotations from *Blackouts to Bright Lights: Canadian War Bride Stories*, edited by Barbara Ladouceur
and Phyllis Spence, are reproduced with the permission of Ronsdale Press Ltd.
Blackouts to Bright Lights was originally published by Ronsdale Press Ltd. in 1995, 5th printing 2007.

Manufactured in the U.S.A.

LIBRARY AND ARCHIVES CANADA CATALOGUING IN PUBLICATION

Piece by piece : stories about fitting into Canada / Teresa Toten, editor.

ISBN 978-0-670-06849-4

1. Immigrants—Canada—Biography—Juvenile literature. 2. Authors, Canadian (English)—20th century—
Biography—Juvenile literature.
I. Toten, Teresa, 1955-

PS8083.P54 2010   jC810.9'0054   C2009-905650-X

Visit the Penguin Group (Canada) website at **www.penguin.ca**

Special and corporate bulk purchase rates available; please see
www.penguin.ca/corporatesales or call 1-800-810-3104, ext. 477 or 474

IN CELEBRATION OF MY FATHER
ADAM VUKOVIC

"They carried their treasures in a crooked box."

NAOMI SHIHAB NYE, "FULL DAY"

CONTENTS

My Piece

TERESA TOTEN

Every single one of us wants, needs, and yearns to belong.

Or ... is it just me?

No. Wanting to belong must be a primal kind of thing, whether we admit it or not. The newly arrived immigrant, like so many young adults, just has a harder time hiding it. Immigrants tend to wear that need on their sleeves, but the rest of us are too busy and distracted by our own yearnings to notice. I believe that this compulsion to "belong" is directly linked to our survival. Our need for community, our search for ourselves, our tribe, our people, is a never-ending quest. Most of us are still looking.

Who hasn't felt alien, isolated, or awkward, often all at the same time? Now stir in the added burden of knowing what was left behind—the aunties, the grandmas, the colours, the aromas ... the *familiar*. No matter how the exit took place, under dire threat or with a sense of adventure, the immigrant always wrestles with memories of some irreplaceable treasures, forever lost.

Those stories are here.

When you think about it, how could an immigrant story *not* be compelling? My own story is, and was, compelling, and I don't even remember it. My father came to Canada as a baby and late in his life went back to Croatia on an extended holiday, where he met and fell in love with my mother. He married her. And then he spent the next two years tirelessly working to bring my mother from Yugoslavia to Canada. Since my mother's family was still being punished by the Communist government of the day, his efforts were useless. Finally, under some pressure from the Canadian government, Yugoslavia issued her a twenty-four-hour exit visa on the day that I was born in Zagreb.

I arrived in Canada on October 26, 1955, on the *Queen Elizabeth II*.

I was thirteen days old.

Six months later my father died.

It was a cruel joke. My mother, bewildered and adrift in a strange land, couldn't cope. The language was impenetrable, there was no family, and there had been no time to make friends. The colours here were too bright and harsh, and the sounds of Canadian life, with all its clamouring machinery and cars, too noisy. And she was alone—well, except for me.

When I was about eight months old, Mama took me to the lake. Literally. She couldn't stand another perplexing, fearful day, wondering how she was going to support us in this cold land. She picked me up, held me tight, and started walking into the still-frigid Lake Erie water. Mama couldn't swim. Icy ripples of water bit into her legs with every step, causing her to stumble and lurch, but she was persistent. My mother was determined to kill us both. When the water reached her waist, she stopped. I slept like a baby throughout this entire ordeal, happy to accommodate whatever she had in mind.

Mama says to this day that it was a "hand of God" kind of thing. She felt pressure on her shoulder, then both her shoulders. Then a whispering. The wind? The wind urged her not to commit this mortal sin, not to risk damning her soul and the soul of her baby for all eternity. "But how ..." The wind told her that it would be okay. That life in Canada would be good.

"Turn around."

And she did.

Mama walked back to shore with a resolve that hasn't faltered in over fifty years. Never mind that because my father was a Canadian citizen, I was immediately deemed a "Canadian Born Abroad." Never mind my dramatic exit and then entry into this country when I was less than two weeks old. I believe that Mama and I were both baptized *Canadian* on that unseasonably cold day in early June, in Lake Erie, Ontario.

As "Canadian" as I am, I've made a career it seems from milking the more outrageous aspects of my Eastern European immigrant roots. Much of my fiction revolves around the themes of "otherness" and, yes, of wanting to "belong." Yet, even as I write about it, I forget what impact those themes may have on my audience. I think I forget I have an audience. When I toured with my two most recent books, *Me and the Blondes* and *Better Than Blonde*, I was met with a phenomenon that both startled me and inspired this anthology.

Time and again, during author signings, one or both of my books would be thrust at me with shaking gloved hands. This would occur more frequently if there was a very long line, which I hasten to add, only happens if you have a nuclear-charged teacher/librarian. "Mrs. Toten," a voice would falter, then regain some urgency. "Mrs. Toten, I don't ... I can't ... I have to tell you how much your book means to me." Since the book was still shaking and the voice still faltering, I would look up and invariably connect with a young woman in full burqa, covered from head to toe, with only a mesh window for her eyes. I confess to being stunned each time it happened.

I guess I "got" why the Blonde books were embraced by blondes, by anyone of Eastern European extraction, and even more generally by anyone from Europe, period. But teens lining up in their burqas and shalwar-kamiz? I finally screwed up the courage to ask a girl in a burqa why. Why did she like the book so much? "Because *I am* Sophie." Enough said, apparently. Sophie Kandinsky is my excitable Bulgarian-Polish heroine. When we meet her Sophie is an outsider because of her culture and family, she is "other" in a brand-new school. And the penny dropped. My "new" Canadian readers were seeing themselves in Sophie's shoes no matter where they came from, no matter what their cultural heritage was. "Other" is other.

Then I started paying attention, real attention, to my audiences in school auditoriums across this country. In most cases almost half the kids in my groups were not born in Canada, and that number rose dramatically when I asked how many of them had parents who were not born in Canada. This was as true for the kids in a Calgary suburb as for high school students in the interior of British Columbia. It was certainly so in all of Toronto and its environs, but also for most parts heading on our way east. Where are their stories? I wondered.

Here.

Every immigrant has a story, and these fourteen stories, each brilliantly told, underline and bring home that truth. I credit or blame my immigrant roots and our constant moving for turning me into a writer. Immigrants are, so often, hyper-aware, hyper-alert to their surroundings. We are alive to every potential snub or slur. We can track a raised eyebrow that is invisible to everyone else at the table. We are forever searching for the unwritten social rules, the clues to belonging.

Those stories are here.

Every immigrant story is a highly idiosyncratic roller coaster of emotions, humiliations, and triumphs, yet most of these pieces at least touch on language as a common flashpoint. It appears that language can be an impenetrable barrier, even when your mother tongue is English!

We begin with a surprise. Svetlana Chmakova's delightful manga story allows us to "see" her learning English from television subtitles and then follow her to ESL class, where she learns to write her name in Mandarin. Svetlana's tale is bookended by Ting-xing Ye's poignant last story, where despite having been an English translator in China, she is stymied by telephone etiquette when trying to apply for a housekeeping job in Canada. To be polite in her new country, should one first ask, "Have you eaten yet?"

Richardo Keens-Douglas grew up speaking English in Grenada. Yet, at nineteen, he had to drum out the troublesome milky rhythms of his island accent in order to "succeed" as a Canadian actor. Rachel Manley also transported herself and her hypnotic Jamaican lilt to an entirely unappreciative audience in Montreal, where she was stalled and perplexed by the language.

Linda Granfield's Boston brogue was so thick, she needed the aid of a helpful "interpreter" at the University of Toronto, and her accent trips her up to this day. Alice Kuipers's English accent never held her back, but some of the actual words morphed and became incomprehensible on their way from her native Manchester to Saskatoon. Still out West, we meet a bewildered nine-year-old Eva Wiseman, fresh from Hungary and plopped uncomprehendingly onto a Winnipeg playground, where she faces a baseball aimed at her head.

Our two writers from India were English speaking, yet only Rachna Gilmore writes about accents both coming and going. Her clipped private-school accent of Mumbai makes way for the plummier tones of London, England, and is modified again to better suit the flatter sounds of Prince Edward Island. Mahtab Narsimhan isn't hampered by accents or English per se, but instead almost drowns in the "alphabet soup" of her first Canadian job in information technology.

Even though our youngest contributor, Boonaa Mohammed, was born in Canada of Ethiopian heritage, his English is shaped by his parents' culture and arguably by the culture of his chosen artistic profession, the muscular world of spoken-word poetry.

Marina Nemat learned English in her native Iran in a gentler time and then enticed her young son to the language with nursery rhymes in a gentler country. Meanwhile, Dimitri Nasrallah segmented his life into Arab, Greek, and English while in the "waiting room" countries of his family's exile, only to find all these languages useless in Montreal.

Finally, Rui Umezawa and Richard Poplak were both English speakers in their teens, but both communicated more vividly, if silently, through the language of American pop culture. Richard was plunked into a multicultural arts school in Toronto directly from apartheid-era South Africa, and Rui came of age in the seventies in Milwaukee, Wisconsin, an experience that was anything but *Happy Days*.

Some of our writers came here for love, some for adventure. Others came to escape horror or deprivation, and still others were the unwitting hostages of determined parents. All had a longing to belong, and all have been enriched by and continue to enrich this country immeasurably. Open this book to any story. Dip in and out at your leisure. I hope you'll find yourself in between the lines and perhaps feel a little less alone. These are fourteen extraordinary journeys. No need to pack your bags—just turn the page.

MY FAMILY MOVED HERE WHEN I WAS JUST ABOUT TO TURN SIXTEEN.

MY MOTHER, MY FATHER, AND MY YOUNGER SISTER.

WHEN WE ARRIVED, ALL WE HAD WERE OUR HASTILY PACKED SUITCASES.

THEY WEREN'T BIG ENOUGH TO FIT EVERYTHING.

WHAT I BROUGHT WITH ME:
CLOTHES, BOOKS, MY BEST DRAWINGS, DIARIES, AND MY STAMP COLLECTION.

WHAT WE LEFT BEHIND:

MY OLDER SISTER, MY HOMETOWN, AND A LIFETIME OF MEMORIES.

HOW DO YOU PACK A LIFE, ANYWAY?...

WE HAD TO BUILD A NEW ONE, PRETTY MUCH FROM SCRATCH.

MY DAD WORKED LONG HOURS AT THE SOFTWARE COMPANY THAT HAD INVITED US TO MOVE.

MY MOM LOOKED AFTER ALL OF US AND MADE SURE WE ALWAYS REMEMBERED WHAT HOME FEELS LIKE.

MY SISTER AND I WENT TO SCHOOL.

EVERYTHING WAS SO NEW AND STRANGE...

...AND WE MUST'VE SEEMED VERY NEW AND STRANGE, TOO.

TO THIS DAY I WONDER, DID PEOPLE MAKE FUN OF US? ENGLISH-IMPAIRED AS WE WERE, WE WOULDN'T EVEN KNOW.

CLASSES WERE TOUGH.

ENGLISHENGLIS
ISHENGLISHENG
ENGLISHENGLIS
HENGLISHEN
SHENGLIS

LUCKILY, THERE WERE TWO THINGS THAT REALLY HELPED ME AND MY SISTER LEARN...

I HAD LEARNED ENOUGH ENGLISH BY THEN TO TALK TO PEOPLE, TO HAVE A CONVERSATION, AND TO UNDERSTAND WHAT THEY WERE SAYING BACK.

WHICH WASN'T ALWAYS A GOOD THING...

SO, RUSSIAN, EH? GOT SOME VODKA YOU WANNA SHARE?

COME ON, IN RUSSIA THAT'S MOTHER'S MILK!

...UM. ...WHAT?

IN RUSSIA, VODKA DRINKS YOU! HAHAHA!

...BECAUSE WE ALL KNOW THAT JOKES BASED ON STEREOTYPES ARE REALLY FUNNY.

(ACTUALLY, NO, THEY AREN'T.)

IN MY SECOND YEAR OF COLLEGE, MY FAMILY BECAME CANADIAN CITIZENS.

CANADA RECOGNIZES DUAL CITIZENSHIP, SO WE WERE ABLE TO KEEP OUR RUSSIAN ONE. TO LOSE THAT WE'D NEED TO SAY WE DIDN'T WANT IT ANYMORE.

WE DIDN'T WANT TO DO THAT.

SO...
    NOW...

...AM I RUSSIAN?

OR AM I CANADIAN?

CANADA...

IT'S MY HOME RIGHT NOW. I LOVE THIS COUNTRY AND THE FRIENDS I MADE HERE.

I LIVE AND WORK HERE, AND I DUTIFULLY PAY TAXES.

WHEN I TRAVEL ABROAD, I USE MY CANADIAN PASSPORT.

BUT THEN... MY RUSSIAN PART SNEAKS UP ON ME.

SVETLANA... ARE YOU FROM RUSSIA?

YES.

Я ТОЖЕ. ВЫ ВСЁ ЕЩЁ РАЗГОВАРИВАЕТЕ?

...ДА! А КАК ДАВНО ВЫ ЗДЕСЬ?

9 ЛЕТ, А ВЫ?...

HEARING SPOKEN RUSSIAN FEELS LIKE WHAT RAIN MUST FEEL TO PARCHED GROUND.

AT OUR HOUSE WE ONLY SPEAK RUSSIAN, AND WE CALL MY OLDER SISTER EVERY WEEK. WE SHARE STORIES, WE LAUGH, WE MISS EACH OTHER.

AND I MISS IT SO VIVIDLY THEN. THE MAPLE TREES IN MY HOMETOWN...

IT SINKS RIGHT IN, MY MOTHER'S LANGUAGE, IT REACHES DEEPER THAN ENGLISH EVER COULD.

YOU KNOW, THEY ARE GREEN.

AND THEY TURN BRIGHT YELLOW IN THE FALL.

THIS BUTTERY GOLD COLOUR, FILTERING THE LIGHT OF THE PALE BLUE SKY.

I DECIDED THIS: I AM RUSSIAN.

AND I AM CANADIAN.

FOR AS LONG AS THESE COUNTRIES WILL HAVE ME AS THEIR CITIZEN.

...AFTER ALL, I DO GET TEASED FOR BOTH.

SO, YOU'RE CANADIAN, EH? WHERE'S YOUR HOCKEY STICK? AND BEAVER HAT?

...

THE END! (?)

Snapshots from the Fringes

RACHNA GILMORE

Mumbai, or As It Was Then, Bombay, 1963

I am in standard four—grade four—in a private girls' school, and first thing this morning our teacher, Mrs. Chaubal, gathers us on the floor in front of her desk so she can read to us. We are a wild, mischievous bunch, and perhaps Mrs. Chaubal hopes a story will calm our high spirits. Clad in our school uniforms— cotton dresses with faint grey-and-white stripes, tied at the waist with sashes—we wriggle against one another. The overhead fan whirrs, creating the movement of air so desperately needed to counter the oppressive Bombay heat. The classroom smells of chalk, antiseptic cleanser, and the rubbery odour of our shoes. But all this fades as Mrs. Chaubal starts to read from a book soon to become one of my absolute favourites—*Anne of Green Gables*.

I am immediately hooked. Not just by a lively character and story, but also by the place, the community in which it is set. I assume it is entirely fictional. I have no inkling that this book is the start of my fitting into a place that will one day be home.

Mrs. Chaubal reads with animation. She is a short, slightly stocky woman with pale skin, reddish hair, and freckles. I don't know where she's from because, to us, all Western accents are weird and indistinguishable from one another. Fodder for huge amusement.

We, of course, speak English with no accent. Or rather, with the "right" accent. Everyone else—foreigners and Indians from the various regions—has a strange accent. Hey, we're Bombayites, part of the most cosmopolitan city in India. We go to one of the best schools, with an international, Western vibe.

In a way, we are on the fringes of both cultures.

Mrs. Chaubal reads to us for half an hour each morning, and when the school year ends, and the novel doesn't, I am so engrossed in it that I have to hunt it down.

I scour the library and the second-hand bookstores where I spend most of my pocket money, to no avail. At last, I get my mother to take me to a new bookstore. I'm overjoyed to find a copy there, and to discover sequels. I save my money until I can afford the book, and I devour it. I buy all the sequels available and read them over and over.

In an uncharacteristic fit of organization, I number my books according to their importance. *Anne of Green Gables* is number one, followed by the sequels. Inside the book I write:

> *The grass is green*
> *The rose is red*
> *This book is mine*
> *'Til I am dead*
> *P.S. Even after I'm dead.*

I don't attempt to articulate then what it is about these books that so delights me, that so works into my inner being. I read for pleasure, and I simply love these books. I am fascinated by Anne's world.

It is so different from mine.

Anne's family life, for instance, and her community, seems so homey, so cozy and intimate, with its predictable, stable rhythms. I am wistfully envious of Anne's chores. Washing dishes! Oh, how delightful, how ... how pioneerish. Imagine the family eating together, and in the kitchen, yet. Imagine living in a community that is familiar, beautiful, and safe, where everyone knows everyone else.

My parents are upper-middle-class Indians, with an active social life, and servants do all the work. My brother and I rarely eat with my parents, and never in the kitchen, which is the servants' domain. I have no chores. My clothes are washed and ironed for me; I order what I want for breakfast, eat what is served for other meals. When we are small, my brother and I have an ayah who looks after us. My idea of housekeeping is, like my mother's, to hold on to the keys to various supplies such as flour and sugar, which are locked up against possible pilfering by servants. It's the only life I know, so it doesn't feel strange, nor do I feel neglected. My parents are loving, but it is, in retrospect, a distant household.

Other aspects of Anne's world also intrigue me—the lack of class distinctions, where farmers are an educated and proud people, not just labourers; the beautiful, serene countryside, so unlike my noisy, vibrant cityscape; the intimacy with nature. I long, like Anne, to walk through the woods in peace and quiet, and see violets and mayflowers. What *are* they? Oh, there are delights in my life that Anne doesn't have, but they are familiar, and taken for granted.

Anne's climate appeals enormously, too. The pressing heat of my world is draining, sapping. When Anne goes for long walks, she doesn't collapse later under a fan, lathered in sweat, her head throbbing from the heat. I've never seen snow, but I long to experience it, and to snowshoe like Anne. I want to be rosy-cheeked and hearty with the cold!

And so, as I read these books over and over, Anne's world becomes almost as familiar as my own. The place and the people, the values—even the stern Protestant work ethic—weave into me.

I'm not sure when I realize that Anne's world is not fictional, that Prince Edward Island is a real place in Canada. Perhaps it's when I study Canada in my geography class and P.E.I. suddenly leaps out.

P.E.I. is real? It's real!

It's a watershed moment. I decide in a burst of exuberance, in a spirit of joyful adventure, that I will go there one day.

I don't think of being Canadian then—not at all—just that one day I will go to P.E.I.

Accents and Constant Threads

I am fourteen. My life is turned upside down when my father gets a job in London, England, and we are to move there. Sure, there is glamour in going abroad, in living in the West, but how will I manage without my friends?

During the long, discombobulating period of packing, I give away my Anne books—my most treasured possessions—to my closest friends. Maybe I think I am growing up and will no longer need them. But it is a wrench.

London. Cooler climate. More orderly than India. Less crowded.

But there are many new challenges.

I have a brief, wretched encounter with stockings—bloody stockings that need bloody garter belts to hold them up—until I discover tights. Tights fit better, way better, than stockings! *I* fit better with tights.

I learn to use the buses and the tube, and find my way around London. And I encounter racism. I am definitely on the fringes by virtue of my colour. I learn a new term—Paki-wog. I am aware of the irony that in India fairness is equated with beauty. And that India and Pakistan, partitioned during Independence, in 1947, are now reunited in England—through scorn. I witness an incident where my father is treated rudely when we eat out at a restaurant, and I hurt for him, for us.

I also adjust to an unfamiliar family closeness as we now eat all our meals together, and in the kitchen! But until the charm fades, I actually relish chores such as cleaning house and washing dishes. It's so ... cozy. So ... Anne-ish.

And, of course, I negotiate the minefield of funny accents.

Oh God, it's *me* this time with the funny accent, although, thank goodness, at least my English is impeccable.

I quickly lose the Indian accent. I mean, really, it just isn't done, not in England. I am encouraged, without its ever being articulated, to become British, to forget every bit about my Indian background ... something best forgotten, really, isn't it, dear?

I don't find that outrageous at the time—after all, I come from a world that is a hangover of colonial rule. I am fourteen and acutely self-conscious. I'm also searching to establish who I am, but most of all, I need to fit.

By the time I visit India again, a year and a half later, I am only mildly embarrassed to be the one with the funny foreign accent because, hey, I now live in swinging London. I represent the glamour and chic of the West in India, even though in actuality I live in the burbs of London, and I am definitely on the fringes.

But during that first visit back, I shamelessly ask my friends to return my Anne books. I didn't realize until the long dry spell in London without them how much they mean to me. They represent a thread of continuity and security in my life. They are old friends. With them I am at ease.

It isn't long before I realize that I can't go back to live in India. I've changed too much. And yet, England isn't right for me either. I have friends, yes, but aside from them, my colour often leaves me in the margins. I smile, pretending I don't care when I am the last girl picked at dances, or am not picked at all. But I do care. I never know when a bus driver or sales clerk will bully me, when racism will wound and blindside me, reducing me to a colour. The incidents aren't frequent, and I am on the whole optimistic and lively, but these experiences do leave internal scars.

When I see Pierre Trudeau on TV, skating, wearing a rawhide jacket with fringes, I am intrigued and charmed—by him and by the Canada he represents. I decide that after I graduate from university, I will travel until I find a place to fit in this world, and I'll start with Canada. Canada seems relaxed and informal. Far less stuffy than Britain. Far more accepting than Britain. Full of possibilities.

Of course, I must go to P.E.I., as I've always dreamed of doing—although with the earnest dignity of a young adult, I am reluctant to admit that a children's book is at the root of this desire.

But P.E.I. appeals also because I've had it with big cities. I want countryside. Community. Dammit, I want to belong. I don't understand or believe my father when he says that there is a flip side to living in small communities.

When I meet, and make friends with, a couple of young people from P.E.I. while youth hostelling in England, it all feels as though it's meant to be.

I'm not in the least nervous about this trip—I am in my early twenties, full of the bravado of youth, eager for adventure. I want to move from the fringes to being in the centre of my life.

In Canada I hope to fit. I hope to belong. To be as comfortable as I am in the Anne books.

Like Anne or Like Tannis?

At first, it's wonderful. I am, at last, living my dream. I am on my own, away from parental authority, and the freedom is delightful. Language is no barrier at all, and hey, I come with the glamour of an English accent, which, for some reason, Canadians love.

P.E.I. is both more and less than I imagined. The culture, in many ways, feels familiar because of the Anne books, although I'm surprised it isn't more like Anne's time. The landscape I love immediately—it is beautiful and instantly familiar. It is home. I look lovingly at the land that Anne gazed at. I love the beaches above all. I go there to relax and heal, to clear the dross of life.

But there are some initial surprises and jolts. The towns and villages seem strangely higgledy-piggledy, unlike quaint English villages. The ugliness of overhead electric wires seems disorderly, and there are oddities such as drive-throughs, and new terms such as *trunk* instead of *boot*; *sidewalk*, not *pavement*; *hamburger*, not *mince*. But it's all part of the fun.

And Canadians *are* so much friendlier than Londoners. More informal and accepting. I have a pack of friends, a guy I meet who is wonderful—whom I later marry—and life is rich, full, and satisfying. I am youthful, optimistic, and enthusiastic, and my delight and exuberance blind me at first to some of the harder realities of the place, and of fitting in.

I immerse myself in the cozy, country type of life I've envied in the Anne books. I buy rocking chairs, knit afghans, make bread by hand, bid for ridiculous items at country auctions, grow vegetables, make jam, and get a kerosene lamp because it's so much more delightful than electric light. I introduce my friends to Indian food, and most of them love the explosion of flavours.

I relish being able to do some of the things Anne does, such as walk through the woods looking for mayflowers, although I am disappointed and surprised that hardly anyone I know in P.E.I. cares about them. And that the mayflowers are a pale comparison to the jasmine I loved in India.

There are other small discrepancies, too, between the Island of the Anne books and my Island. Anne and Marilla sat outside on their doorstep for hours, gazing at the sunset. How come *they* weren't eaten alive by mosquitoes and blackflies? Why is there no mention in the Anne books of bloody blackflies?

These are the first small clues that my romantic perceptions of P.E.I. may not withstand reality. That the happy, accepting community I envisioned isn't quite as it seems. That although I've chosen Canada and married an Islander, although I feel that I am where I want to be, where *I* want to belong, not everyone here feels that accepting of *me*.

You don't just fit because you *want* to. There is a process, and it's not always easy.

Life isn't like a storybook, not even in P.E.I.

Once the initial euphoria and sense of adventure begin to wear off, I reluctantly start to see that although Canada is more tolerant and open than Britain, there is still racism and xenophobia here, both overt and covert.

Reality slowly, slowly, starts to creep in.

I have advantages that many newcomers don't have— language isn't an issue as it is for some, and I have an in, having married an Islander.

But.

There is the friend of my husband who tells us how his grandmother said she was so disappointed when she'd heard that my husband had married an Indian girl, but after she met me, she was so impressed.

Wow. Gee thanks.

There is the rumour that circulates back to us that my husband and I had an arranged marriage. We're dumbstruck by where that could possibly have originated.

There are other incidents, slights small and large.

But there are also funny moments. My husband's elderly grandmother, whom I enjoy greatly, blurts out one time, "Well, we're all the same colour in the dark." My husband and I crack up over this. It doesn't sting because I know she genuinely likes me.

But.

There is a discrepancy between my embrace and love of this land, this country, between my identification with it and the willingness of some of the locals to accept me. There is a divide, a gap in the reality, between our perceptions.

As my accent shifts yet again from English to Canadian—hey, accents are my thing, and part of coming home is acquiring the right accent—my identity, to those who first meet me, is increasingly informed by my skin colour.

Many people can accept that, but some can't. It's unexpected and it wounds.

I encounter, and am bewildered by, Canada's multicultural policy. Its purpose appears laudable, but it seems to want to slot me into a category, name me Indian, and encourage me to embrace "Indian" culture. To showcase it, even.

Except I don't label or separate what is "Indian" in me—it's all woven into who I am as an individual.

Anyway, there isn't one Indian culture; India has dozens of languages and cultures, fluid and changing, and my

Westernized outlook is part of it too, part of Bombay culture.

There is no single, right way to be an immigrant.

I discover to my surprise and discomfort, both in P.E.I. and later in Ottawa, Canadians of Indian heritage who embrace their version of Indian culture with a rigidity that renders it a frieze of a culture that no longer exists in India. I am not Indian enough for them, either, but nor do I want to fit there.

I am puzzled, in my search for who I am, and how to fit here, as to who I *should* be.

To some, I'm considered not Indian enough, not exotic enough. There is the white acquaintance who tells me I'm neglecting my culture. To others who are uncomfortable with the colour of my skin, whether they hide it or shout Paki-wog— and yes, this happens, even in friendly P.E.I.—I am too Indian, too different.

I teeter between guilt and confusion because I don't feel particularly Indian, because I'm not more Indian, and resentment at having cultural assumptions thrust upon me.

Why do I need to explain my lack of sufficient Indianness to anyone, because, for God's sake, who goes about telling white Canadians that they are not Scots/French/Irish/Polish/ Ukrainian enough?

I want to name myself. I want the term *Canadian* to include me as I am.

Belonging is something you can't take for granted if you aren't born here.

It dawns on me that in P.E.I., I am still on the fringes. The other, not in. I have friends with whom this isn't an issue, but at times I find myself dislocated, jolted when I least expect it—at the party when I am the only one to object to a racist joke. Afterwards, as I talk about it on the phone with a close friend, who cries with me, I yank at a hangnail on my little toe. It rips. I'm surprised at how it bleeds.

I come to realize that in Anne's world, I'd be regarded as Tannis of the Flats, a character in one of Montgomery's stories who is First Nations, although L.M.M. calls her Indian. She is the other. The wild one, who by her blood is considered savage. When I read that story first in India, I feel pain and uneasiness because I see that is how I'd be perceived in a world in which I want to belong. I dislike the story and shove it to the back of my mind. I am also outraged that First Nations people, who were here first, should be depicted so callously as the other.

When you read a book, you are no colour.

I discover, too, the flip side of the small community that my father warned me about—the undercurrents of gossip, the lack of privacy, all further complicated by my being perceived as different.

I find the racism harder to weather when I have children, the time I hear a child whisper of my daughter, "Oh my God, she's black." Slights against my kids leave me far more enraged, fearful, helpless, and pierced through the heart than any attack on me.

When? When do you belong?

Slowly, I come to understand that in P.E.I., anyone who isn't born and bred there is from "away," although in a community lacking cultural diversity, visible minorities stand out more.

I come to understand, too, that it isn't just race that excludes people—everyone feels on the outside at times. It isn't okay, but it makes me feel less singled out.

I become wary now of the term *kindred spirit* from the Anne books, because I see that for every person who is included in that inner circle, more are excluded.

And yet ...

For every act of exclusion, careless or deliberate, well-meaning or malicious, there are many acts of inclusion, of hands held out in friendship. Of community support. Of genuine warmth and connection.

With my eyes now wide open to the realities of this place—it is not Anne's world; it is what it is—I go through a long, slow process of trying to find the niche in which I fit.

It is tied inextricably with finding myself, with fitting in *me*.

It is tied with at last starting to write.

I soon discover that many writers are on the outside. From the fringes. It's from here that you can best observe—it has distinct advantages. That outsider status can be a gift.

Snapshots of Belonging

It's difficult to come up with only a few snapshots of belonging because mostly I do belong. Canada and I have grown and evolved together, so that belonging is a status that is rarely jolted now, although it does still happen.

Even so, there are *aha* and *wow* moments of belonging, of fitting, of triumph and success. Of really coming home.

When ... I am invited by the L.M. Montgomery Conference, in P.E.I., to be a keynote speaker. Sometimes life *is* neater than fiction.

When ... in a bookstore at the site of L.M. Montgomery's homestead in P.E.I., I see a child absorbed in a book—my first book.

When ... I am invited to speak at international conferences as a writer from Canada.

When ... one of my books wins the Governor General's Award for Children's Literature.

When ... I come home to Canada, after a difficult trip abroad, and the young, pink-faced passport officer says, "Welcome home." And God, it's so *good* to be home where I belong.

You're Not from
Around Here, Are You?

LINDA GRANFIELD

I didn't flee some cataclysmic event in my homeland. The earth
didn't open its maw to swallow my village. No missiles hailed
down from the cloudy skies and destroyed my ancestors'
pastures. Enemy troops were not quartered in my family's
home, eating all our food and plundering our traditions and
wealth. My freedom to say what I believed was never denied. No
duress made me emigrate from the United States of America.

I came to Canada to go to university.

It's that simple a reason. No war. No disease. No limitation of
freedoms. And if I'd had more than thirty dollars to invest in
graduate school applications in 1974, I might never have arrived
in Toronto.

I'd decided to carry on with my education, and a professor in
Boston, Massachusetts, encouraged me to continue with my
major in Victorian literature. I wanted to study the books
written by people like Charles Dickens and Marie Corelli.
Nothing I researched would bring world peace, find a cure for
cancer, or develop eco-friendly environments. But these
further studies were quite serious to me, and I had only thirty

dollars to send as an application fee. That would finance one application. But which one?

My professor first suggested a university in California. No, too far away from Massachusetts; I wanted to be closer to home. How about the University of Toronto? Fine Victorian studies program, he stated. My response? "Where's Toronto?"

"Where's Toronto?" By uttering that question then, and writing it here today, I feed some of the very anti-Americanism I found when I first arrived at the Toronto airport and continue to find today. My acceptance into the graduate program at the University of Toronto did not guarantee my acceptance into Canada's embrace.

So how much did I know about Canada?

I knew that French was spoken in Quebec because my Greater Boston radio picked up a Montreal station and I listened in, hoping to improve my high school French. I knew there was a province (not a state) that had a name like the peach. You know, Alberta peaches. In a can. Not even from Alberta, Canada. In my defence, I never believed that all Canadians lived in igloos.

I didn't think of myself as an immigrant to Canada when I arrived, alone, at Toronto's airport, ready to begin my new life. Anyone seeing the gear I brought with me might have thought differently. A taxi took me to my new address, a rooming house near beautiful High Park. When the cab pulled away, I was standing, alone, with my few belongings: two orange towels, two orange pots, and some late-summer clothing (not orange). Suddenly, all my courage left me and I fought back tears. I didn't know one person in the city. Or in all of Canada.

Among my mother's parting words in Boston had been expressions of encouragement, support, and comfort, or so she thought.

"Don't worry," Mum said. "It's not like you're going to a foreign country. They're just like us."

I soon learned how wrong my mother was.

The money, the postal deliveries, the grocery brands—all different. But language, or the differences between "Canadian" and "American" English, was the major obstacle I met. I didn't write graduate seminar papers spelling words properly with *u* (*humour*, *colour*, etc.). I asked for a napkin in a neighbourhood restaurant—the butter tart, my first, was delicious and drippy. I got a puzzled look from the waiter. Did I mean "serviette"? I guess so—I had to wait and see what a serviette was. Damn! It was a—napkin!

It's easy to look back and chuckle at how language was an issue for me as a newcomer to Canada. In my university class someone actually acted as a translator for me when I pronounced the word *martyr* with my Boston Irish accent. Dropped *r*'s and flat *a*—*mahtah*. I had to repeat the line three times for the professor. That's when the "translator" stepped in. Much laughter ensued.

"Just like us," my mother had said. Really?

I've found there are variations of the inevitable question I get whenever I meet a new group of Canadians. It's abruptly asked a few minutes into the conversation, accompanied by a tilt of the head and a smirk of a smile, "Do I detect an accent?" Or, "Don't tell me. Let me guess. You're from New York?" which is particularly insulting to a *Bostonian!*

Or, and always, "You're not from around here, are you?"

The only place I've found in Canada where I am never pegged as American for the way I speak is Nova Scotia. There, probably as a result of cross-border transit by New Englanders and their kin, I'm asked if I'm from Clark's Harbour (pronounced *Clahk's Hahbah*), a town on Nova Scotia's south shore.

And I *am* a Canadian. Now.

But it wasn't always thus. I had to learn how this country, despite my mother's claim, was *not* just like the United States. I've always liked history, so I found delving into the Acadian expulsion and "meeting" Louis Riel, the voyageurs, and Banting and Best enjoyable. I have loved the research, every hour spent in museums, each author visit that took me into a new-to-me community.

From the start of my university days in Toronto I embraced all things Canadian: that gooey butter tart, poutine, moose meat, beaver tails. The governor general, the prime minister, the Members of Parliament. I read the national newspaper, watched the news on the CBC, and tried to speak French, again with little luck. I wore a poppy on Remembrance Day, not Memorial Day. I celebrated both July first and fourth but had to hoard fireworks from Canada (Dominion) Day for my backyard celebration on the Fourth, when it was just me, some ice cream, and a few dazzling sparklers in the dark.

When I went back to visit my family during university breaks, I "bought Canadian" and talked about how great it was "up there."

My efforts to become more like Canadians themselves, however, were slim to none during my student days. After all, I was attending university for only two years. Then I'd move back home and work on the thesis to finish my degree. My time in Canada would be just one short chapter in my life's story.

Someday, I guessed, I would tell my grandchildren about the incredible time I spent in Toronto, already a city of many cultures in the seventies. I'd share how I took the train to

Montreal and the bus to Niagara Falls. How I'd eaten food from around the world. How I'd seen Gordon Lightfoot perform. How Canadians were, on the whole, nice people, except when they got in my face about the way I spoke.

Other issues, however, became prickly points during my student days in Canada. I found I had to be careful whenever U.S. politics came up over coffee, because Americans were "the enemy." I was told that the Americans wanted to own Canada. News to me. During particularly rabid anti-American discussions, usually someone would quickly look over at me and say, "Oh sorry, I don't mean *you*. Some of my best friends are Americans." I knew there was no chance they'd think of inserting "Polish," "Jewish," or "Italian" in place of "American." Feeling peer pressure, I seldom made an issue of the offensive comments. I wish I had.

I got what I came to Canada for: those incredible classes and professors; life in a huge, vibrant city; and eventually the graduate degree. But I also found something else, something I hadn't planned on, and that was ... love.

I know, I know. How corny and squishy is that? She found love!

Yep. In one of my courses. In fact, in the class where *martyr* was translated for me. Tall, dark, handsome, born-in-Toronto, smart-as-a-whip, poutine-eatin', hockey-lovin' Cal. Suddenly, everything changed. I'd never stopped to think about life *forever* away from my American home. I'd never considered what it would be like to continually face what was clearly a national dislike, bordering on hatred, for my land of birth. I was in love. *My* Canadian was terrific. All would be well.

Simple paperwork enabled me to come to Toronto to study, but authorization of another sort was needed if I were to marry a Canadian. I had to be sponsored by my husband-to-be. I had to have medical tests and lots of legal documents completed. There was the required interview with the official in the Canadian government's Boston office. Marriage didn't guarantee legal entry into Canada.

I felt lower than a snake's hips the day I walked into Monsieur Bibeau's waiting room. What if he refused to accept my application? The wedding date had been set, the reception menu (pot roast and French green beans) planned and booked, and I was already making my dress. Panic set in. What if Canada said, gulp, no?

I saw only one other applicant for entry to Canada that day. An exotic dancer from Haiti. She spoke French. And when she left the waiting area for her interview, the office administrators giggled, "Une danseuse exotique!" I wondered if being *une étudiante americaine*, soon to be *une mariée* would be equally hilarious to them. More nerves; more sweat. What if there was a quota that day? Who would make the cut?

I did. Maybe the dancer from Haiti did too. The waiting room was empty when I left the office.

Just before my wedding, my mother told me I was taking the family "back to Canada." What?! Yes, I had grandparents, long gone and never mentioned, who had emigrated from New Brunswick to Massachusetts. The words *going home* became even more confusing. Where was I headed? Where was home?

If *home* meant where we are most comfortable, it would become increasingly difficult to call Canada home. As long as I kept quiet, didn't speak, I could blend in with other white Canadians. The minute I spoke, however, I identified myself via an accent Canadians claimed to know thanks to American television programs. As usual, they identified me as a New

Yorker. Once in a while, a Canadian who watched the popular show *Cheers*, about friends in a Boston bar, got it right. A heated discussion of why Canadians had so many American shows to watch usually ensued.

Being an "American abroad" became a larger issue. The longer I lived in Canada, the more awkward it became when I heard the glowing attributes that Canadians believed defined them in the world—an excess of politeness and a reluctance to speak up for oneself. Despite all the lovely examples of genuine friendship and generosity I encountered, I found too many occasions of rudeness, racism cloaked in supposed humour, and aggression.

I know the stereotype of the "ugly American" has long been alive in the world, not just in Canada. When I first came here, the Vietnam War was still raging, and among my fellow students were draft dodgers—American youths who left the United States rather than fight in a war they could not support. Some Canadians were upset that these Americans had crossed the border, had taken jobs, and lived "underground." The fall of Saigon in 1975 didn't help matters, as the dodgers were front-page news in Canada's newspapers.

While my neighbours in Toronto were quick to say that they loved the friendliness of Americans when they travelled in the States for their vacations, this warm, fuzzy feeling was forgotten when they returned home. Soon the travel stories evolved into the old rants.

After we had our children to love and protect, I felt more uncomfortable in the country I'd chosen to live in. I watched the Japanese and Greek communities in Toronto celebrate their traditional holidays in city streets and parks. I noticed that the American community didn't celebrate anything in public. In fact, they/we hid. Why? Because we were representatives of politics that were despised. A Fourth of July picnic in High Park wasn't worth putting our children in danger when protesters arrived.

Many Americans in Canada stopped raising a U.S. flag in their yard on their traditional holidays. I put the American flag up, but I have to admit I was surprised when it was still there and our house wasn't egged by the end of the day. I refused to be cowed by the anti-American sentiments—my children had a right to celebrate their heritage.

The tolerance I'd expected to find when I immigrated wasn't here. I couldn't protect my children from every anti-American diatribe they encountered in the media or in the schoolyard. The joke/insult of "your mother wears army boots" actually became "your mother's an American" during the Gulf War in 1991. I visited schools to present the history books I wrote. As the Gulf War dragged on, the students' questions became more bewildering: "Why do Americans like war so much?" or "Do you wish you weren't American?" These children were ten to twelve years old! This ingrained dislike of Americans was so deep that I heard it from young children who didn't even *know* someone from the United States.

During the Gulf War, I had two brothers serving in the United States Army as career soldiers. Security issues meant that my family could not know where those brothers, my kids' uncles, were. Our children wrapped a yellow ribbon, a now-traditional symbol of hope for a safe return, around the tree in our front yard. It disappeared overnight. We put out another. It too was taken.

The taunting at school and the front-yard vandalism were upsetting and hurtful for us all. I had imagined that the longer I lived here and the more time and energy I invested in my community, the better I'd feel. Instead, I realized I was living in fear in my adopted country.

It has always been difficult to ignore the intolerance and

disrespect I encounter: the boos I hear when the American national anthem is played at sports events; the "I am Canadian" beer ad rant that was directed at my native land; Rick Mercer's smug "Talking to Americans" program that is repeatedly televised to amuse the Canadian audiences who, I guess, feel they know everything about the United States.

By now, you might be getting a little ticked off at me. Bitch, bitch, bitch ... if she was so unhappy here, why didn't she move back to the United States? Why is she still here?

I'm still here because I *wanted* to become a Canadian. There was nothing logical about that decision. It was purely emotional. I had built connections to Canada and its people while experiencing it at its worst and its best. I was bringing up my children in classrooms filled with children of immigrants like myself, from over one hundred nations.

I had seen Canada's geography from sea to sea and loved it: the majestic Rocky Mountains; the mists of Vancouver Island; the Blood Reserve in Alberta; the *Bluenose II* in Halifax Harbour. I was able to have the writing career I'd always wanted. And, in some strange way, I felt I was already a Canadian.

I'll admit that more than once I considered going for some accent-purging class that would help me find those lost r's—but in the end, admittedly often angrily, I decided other Canadians had to accept me as I am.

My landed immigrant status paper, a bubble-gum pink document, had given me all the rights and privileges my Canadian husband enjoyed, except for voting. There was irony in the fact that I was visiting schools with my book *Canada Votes*. I was explaining the electoral process to future Canadian voters. Yet I couldn't vote!

I remember *exactly* when I knew it was time for me to become a full-fledged citizen. June 1996. On a moonlit night on Parliament Hill in Ottawa, no less! As a "Canadian" author, I had been invited to lunch with the Speaker of the Senate. That evening, as I strolled alone and gazed at the full moon rising behind the Peace Tower, it hit me. "I want to become a citizen." No warning. Just a crystal-clear, emotional wallop. Just *whack!*

It was time to become a Canadian, with all rights and privileges and duties. My children and my husband were Canadians. I was writing and sharing Canadian history. My parents had both passed away in 1995, and, while they never expressed an opinion either way about my taking Canadian citizenship, I felt a certain release and freedom to do so. Gradually, ties to one home had weakened, and bonds to Canada had become tighter than ever.

I drove back to Toronto. I'd made my decision and I was in a hurry! No stopping now, no turning back! I drove the next day to a government office to apply for citizenship. I even got a parking space—a good omen if ever there was one! Hurry to the elevator! Hurry to the application desk! Pen ready! That pink status paper in hand! "Can I help you?" the official at the desk smiled and asked. Yes!

I was shocked when I heard the process would take two years. "Why so long?" I asked. "There are *six thousand* applications ahead of yours," she said, still smiling.

When you are born in Canada, perhaps you never think about *why* others want to become Canadians. You don't know whether war, famine, cruel government regimes, jobs, or love drives people to Canada's shores. You might not know the steps people take to become citizens. There are rules to be followed. Years to be lived in Canada. And tests to be taken.

The written tests are not easy, even for someone like me who has English as a first language and who writes about Canada. I heard a lot of weeping in the room before, during, and after I took my citizenship test because people were afraid of failing, of not becoming the Canadians they wish to be, perhaps of even moving backwards, instead of forwards, on their life's path.

Nearly two years after I first applied, my family watched as I spoke the words that legally made me a Canadian. "Don't worry," Mum had said all those years ago to the frightened me. "They're just like us." Maybe my mother wasn't entirely wrong, as I first supposed. Canadians and Americans share a continent, my ancestors were part of the history of both nations, and my children live, as thousands do, in a binational family. I was "bringing" my New Brunswick ancestors back to Canada.

I can laugh at the decisions I must make sometimes, for example, during the Olympics. Which country's team will I cheer for? Both, for I *am* both. Now, I get defensive when I hear American media criticize Canadian culture or policy. Or if a Massachusetts friend blames us (Canadians) for all the cold weather that "you're sending down here." I have to remind that friend that Toronto and Boston are virtually on the same latitude and I'm not really "up north."

I chuckle when I read about American plans to build walls between our two nations to keep out the terrorists. I react as a Canadian. Now, I defend as well as criticize Canada. I sincerely want to contribute all I can to this country in whatever way I can. Corny and squishy again, but true.

Still, in my weaker, less placid moments, I get fired up by what I see on the television or read in the papers nearly every day, the intolerant words that slam my traditions and my ethnic heritage. In those moments, I don't believe that my feelings of vulnerability will ever totally disappear. I may celebrate one, Canadian Thanksgiving, but steadfastly, I will set off fireworks on July first *and* July fourth.

Sometimes, when I'm caught up in daily life, I forget where I came from. I'm just like other people, working, having some fun, figuring out my life. And then, suddenly, as happened during the months I worked on this essay, something happens. I feel the sting again.

On a frigid January night, at about ten o'clock, the train pulled into Toronto's Union Station. I'd been to Montreal to visit our daughter. Ice covered the steps descending from the train car, and I was afraid of tumbling to the platform with my heavy suitcase. I called to the railway employee who was standing at the bottom of the steps in order to help passengers. He was chatting to a fellow employee across the platform.

I called, "Hello!" to get his attention. The station was noisy with the steam, the idling engine, and many passengers. He didn't seem to hear me. I called again. He grabbed my suitcase out of my hand, and I safely stepped off the train. As I thanked him and began to hurry off, I was suddenly aware of his angry voice. He began to yell at me, saying I hadn't thanked him, that I shouldn't have called him, that I was rude, and so on.

I was tired from the long journey and totally surprised by what I was hearing. I looked around. Yes, he *was* yelling at me! I asked him what else he had wanted as I'd already thanked him.

He kept on yelling. Other passengers ignored all of this and moved to the escalator nearby.

Suddenly, I heard another voice coming from the dark, from the fellow's friend, who was leaning against a nearby post. "You have yourself a happy Martin Luther King Day!" he snorted. Then he laughed long and hard.

I wondered what Martin Luther King Jr. Day had to do with anything. I, a Canadian, hadn't even realized it was an American holiday. It took me a few seconds to realize what he meant. I cannot describe the anger I felt. An ethnic slur had hurtled through the cold winter air toward me that night.

"Do I detect an accent?"

"They're just like us," Mum had said.

And, after thirty-five years in Canada, I still wonder. What *ever* happened to that exotic dancer from Haiti?

What Is for You, Is for You

RICHARDO KEENS-DOUGLAS

The very first thing I was told was that I had to lose my accent. Why? Why did I have to lose my beautiful lilt? It was the accent of my mum, my teachers, my neighbours, my prime minister— of everyone I loved. What was wrong with the way I talked? I *liked* my accent!

See, from the day I was born I knew exactly what I wanted to do with my life, and that in itself was a blessing. I grew up on a lush little island in the Caribbean called Grenada, which is known for its nutmeg; as a matter of fact, it is affectionately called the Isle of Spice. As a young man, I found life on the island magical, with its rivers, waterfalls, crystal-clear blue sea to swim in, and fruits in abundance. It was pure joy! It sounds like paradise, and well, to be quite honest, it was. Yet, despite the enchantment surrounding me, my world was one of the imagination. The only thing I knew as a young boy was that I wanted to perform. I wanted to be in the theatre—to be an actor. As a child, I would go to the movies and when I got home, lock myself in my room and act out all the characters I had just seen on the screen. My room became the setting for many little worlds, and all belonged to me.

One day, when I was fourteen, I decided to form a local dance group with some of my friends. My neighbour had just come back from New York, where she had seen a show called the Ice Follies. She knew how much I loved the theatre, so she brought me back a program with all the fantastic pictures of the costumes and sets from the show. I decided to call my newly formed company the Spice Follies. That was the beginning of my journey into the world of the performing arts. It seemed as easy as eating a mango pie. Little did I know!

I never liked regular school. I found it unnecessary to learn Latin and algebra when all I wanted to do was act onstage. "If only there were a performing school on this little rock in the middle of the Caribbean Sea," I always said, "I would be the happiest boy on earth."

I was lucky to have parents who encouraged me to do what I wanted to do. When they realized that my heart was set on performing, and there was no way of learning any of that "drama stuff" on the island, they sent me to Montreal to study theatre. I was nineteen, and I will never forget the surprise when I landed in Canada. I came out of the terminal into the cold winter air, opened my mouth to talk, and was shocked to see mist exiting my mouth like smoke. I panicked, thinking my insides were on fire, and began to breathe heavily, wondering what on earth was going on inside me. I needed a drink of water! Then I looked up and saw it was snowing. I gingerly held a snowflake in my hand and squeezed it. I couldn't believe I was actually touching snow. It was as if I had discovered white gold that fell from the heavens.

I auditioned and got into the three-year program at Dawson College, Dome Theatre.

The drama teachers' insistence on changing the way I talked was another surprise. They told me if I wanted to be successful in the "real theatre world," I had to speak like a North American and acquire something called the transatlantic accent, which is supposed to be neutral. But as far as I was concerned, it was in the middle of nowhere, bland and empty, with no soul. A Caribbean person is *not* neutral. We are very expressive and musical in the way we talk. There is a certain rhythm, a spirit, to our speech and movement that enhances everything we do. But the teachers insisted that with that accent of mine, I would find work only in a play set on a Caribbean island. At first I was insulted—I wanted to give them a good piece of Caribbean talk that would really put them in their place—but then I remembered that I wanted to be an actor, and this was all part of the process.

So, my first and main goal in Canada was to change the way I sounded. You should have heard me: "Ahhhhh—ouuuu, couuuuu, moooo." I sounded like I needed to go to the bathroom in a hurry. I had to do tongue twisters really fast to improve my diction: "A big black bug bit a big black bear made a big black bear bleed black bug"; "Peter Piper picked a peck of pickled peppers; a peck of pickled peppers Peter Piper picked." All I could think was that if my friends back home could hear me, they would definitely put me in a straitjacket. After three years of training and trying to find this new sound that was supposed to help me survive and succeed, to bring me a pot of gold as an actor, I graduated.

Now I was out in the "real theatre world" with my new-found Canadian twang, drama training, and technique. I was twenty-two, prepared, and ready like Freddy. I was going to be a star—to take Canada by storm. Everyone would read about me in the newspapers, and not because I was going to jail.

My name would be up in lights.

I had no idea.

I started going to auditions for commercials, movies, and TV shows. I quickly noticed that all the parts I was getting were that of a slave, a pimp, or some other low-life character. I never got to audition for the roles I saw in the movies when I was a little boy, like the character who falls in love with the beautiful girl and rides off into the sunset, the notes of an incredible music score swelling beneath him. No way. I was always riding off in the back of a police van with the sound of sirens blaring and blinking lights, or being killed in the first five minutes of the movie. I remember telling some friends to go see me in this new movie I was so proud of, and they came five minutes late, just in time to see me being carried out on a stretcher, dead. And that was my big scene.

It slowly started to sink in that maybe all that masterful training and technique I got in theatre school didn't really matter. What seemed to matter was my colour and my accent, which I thought I had lost but must have kept creeping into the crevices of my speech. And, well, my colour—there was very little I could do about that.

But I am stubborn, and I wanted it bad. So I continued with my dream. I stayed focused and kept my vision right in front of me. In my worst moments, I could hear my mother saying, "What is for you, is for you." No matter what, if you are destined to be an actor and you keep at your dream, it will happen. And acting in Canada was my dream.

One day, I was called out of the blue to audition for a musical in Toronto called *The Boyfriend*, set in the twenties. It was about young people falling in love in the south of France. Now you know, there was no way that in the twenties, a black man would ever be the boyfriend of a white girl, but the director, God bless him, didn't care. He hired me because I was the best for the role.

The show was a smash hit.

With the success of the play, I invited an agent to come see me perform, in hopes of her becoming my manager. The very next day, we met in her office. From the moment I entered, I heard nothing but praise for my work. She loved the show, thought I was the best thing on the stage, etc., etc., and then all of a sudden, she turned to me and exclaimed, "If only I could dip you in bleach!"

"Huh?" I said. Did I hear right? Did she say she would love to dip me in bleach? I must have looked stunned. I *was* stunned.

The agent had a wonderful smile on her face. "You know, bleach, like the stuff you whiten clothes with?" She gave me a warm laugh, and I knew in her heart she meant well. She was not trying to hurt me. In fact, in her own creative, naive way, she was being honest. What she was saying was, if only you were white, it would be so easy to get you work. Okay. So maybe I knew she didn't mean to be awful.

But bleach?

I found another agent. I kept going. The journey cannot end with someone trying to bleach me and hang me out to dry.

I auditioned and was accepted into the Stratford Shakespearean Festival. It was a great time in my life. I enjoyed every moment. Living in Stratford was like a fairy tale. It was a small town, the people were nice, and the scenery was quaint. I found real magic there. Magic, like back home. Maybe I felt at home because I came from a small island, and Stratford's pace was closer to Grenada's tranquil, easygoing style. I used to sit by the Avon River and watch the swans glide elegantly along. It was a perfect getaway from the hustle and concrete of Toronto.

Getting into such a prestigious company is what every young actor dreams about. There were three of us black actors at the time, out of a company of one hundred or so. Unlike the white actors, we were consistently given walk-on parts, or the roles of the forest lord lurking behind a tree or the foot soldier bringing up the rear of one of good old England's kings. I was never a Romeo or a Macbeth. Still, there is an old saying in the theatre, "There are no small actors, only small roles," so I kept that comforting thought in my mind and trotted on.

Somehow, I was given the daunting opportunity to under-study one of the lead actors in a major production, and as fate would have it, he got sick and I had to take his place. I was elated, thrilled at the chance to prove my brilliance on the big stage at the Festival Theatre! I phoned my friends and told them the good news, and they were all so proud of me. I wanted every-body on my little island to know what a son of the soil was doing. Then a couple of days later, much to my surprise, they offered the role to someone else who was not even the understudy.

I couldn't begin to understand why. How could that happen to me? It didn't make any sense. It was *wrong*. I was the under-study; therefore, it was only right that I should get the role. Finally, it got back to me that the director couldn't stomach the idea of a black person playing the part. "Blacks do not *do* Shakespeare!" he said.

I was devastated.

It was so unjust. I wanted to quit, to give them all a piece of my mind, and not the nice piece, but sometimes you have to bend a little, not break, and move on and see what you can get out of the situation. So I tried to put it behind me by hearing my mum's voice: "What is for you, is for you." And so said, so done. Two days later, the actor who had been given the role also got sick, and who had to go on? *Moi*.

I went on and did my thing and was a great success.

At the end of each season, the artistic director met individually with the actors to let them know their roles in the upcoming season, and again I was offered nothing decent, just walk-ons. It was very disappointing. I was much too ambitious to spend another nine months dressing a stage with my body and suppressed talent. So I left.

Once back in Toronto, I kept going. I took classes to better myself, and went to hundreds and hundreds of auditions. It's what an actor does, especially a Canadian actor. After a while, I started getting good roles, roles that had nothing to do with colour or accents, that dealt with people, their emotions and situations.

But something had changed within me. I started feeling different. I just couldn't put my finger on exactly *how*.

I was happy. Wasn't I?

Finally, I was getting good parts in the theatre. Yet, I couldn't shake off the feeling that something was off balance, missing. Then one day, as I lay in my bed, it hit me like a coconut falling from a tree. It was like a new awakening. I realized that I was not being myself. Somehow, slowly and quite unconsciously, I had been drawn into the game of trying to "fit in" and was trying to be somebody else. I was trying to fit into what society, friends, and Canada wanted me to be.

Who I really was, was going up in smoke, and fast. The little boy who used to run so freely on the beach back in Grenada, climb the mountains, skip river stones, and fill a room with his laugh was no more. The little boy who was ambitious enough to form a dance group at age fourteen and put on his own show to a packed house was disappearing into that "transatlantic" sound, into a quasi-Canadian actor.

The young man who was not afraid to speak up, who never worried about the way he sounded, was becoming meek. I was suppressing all the things that made me, me. In order to "fit in," to "not make waves," I checked the things that made me unique and different. Nothing was spontaneous for me anymore. My whole life was like a well-rehearsed play. I scrutinized the way I sounded and expressed myself because I was led to believe that to be part of it all, to be a Canadian success, I had to give up the most important thing of all: myself. For years this meant that I was embarrassed by my culture, my heritage, my mother and father, and the list began to grow endlessly just because I wanted so much to be accepted, to be a success.

Ironically, I was working; I was a success and I was lost. I was banking too much on my talent and too little on my Grenadian soul.

At a party with my old friends from the islands, I actually felt like two people: one who longed to be just me, and the other who felt lost from yearning so hard to be accepted in this new world called Canada. I did not know which one I should pull out of the bag to relate to everyone around me. It was exhausting. My soul was getting tired. I felt as if I were dragging around two people in this little brown body. Then one day, I got up and said, "Canada, this is me. Accept me for who I am. Accept the way I look, the way I speak, and the spirit of my soul. And if you can't accept me for me, well, that is your problem not mine."

The moment I said it, a weight was lifted off my shoulders. Maybe because for the first time in a long time, I was in charge of me again. I took back control of *me* from the directors, the agents, the reviewers, and even well-meaning friends.

I went back to what I knew best, what was in my heart. I started writing my own stories and plays. I wrote about my experiences, and feelings and thoughts, and pain and laughter and love, and what made me tick. I started being proud once again of what was placed in me from birth.

A whole new world opened up to me because I had found my voice again, one that had never really been heard the way it should have in Canada, but is now. It's a voice that was and is different, with a beautiful cadence and a Grenadian accent that could only be mine. If I was still ashamed of who I was, and scared of what people thought or said about me, my individuality would not have flourished. I would still be in a corner trying to be somebody else just to please other people who don't give two hoots about me. Instead, I have written books and plays, hosted television shows, worked in the theatre, and dined with prime ministers and princes and princesses—all with a lilt in my voice.

I first came to Canada when I was nineteen with all my dreams. Soon, I got lost in a strange world and left my soul behind. Then, somehow, at thirty I found my way out of that place and landed for the second time in Canada with my soul and my dreams intact. That second entry, that rebirth, happened only when I finally figured out that to be a success, you have to be yourself. Yes, my mum was right, "what is for you, *is* for you," but you'd better figure who you are first.

One Foot
in the Future

ALICE KUIPERS

If I'd thought about it at all, I'd have thought moving to Canada would be easy. Lots of people have immigrated there before me, most Canadians speak English, they're known for their friend-liness—how hard could it be? But I didn't think about it because moving to Canada was never part of my life plan. Falling in love with a Canadian wasn't the future I saw for myself. But that's what happened.

In Britain during the Second World War, thousands of British women met and fell in love with Canadian soldiers. "Dressed in their uniforms looking big, smart, beefy—they were gorgeous," is how my granny puts it, remembering the Canadian soldiers who were stationed in London. "But, ooohh, how they complained about the damp."

Once the soldiers had met their British girls, quick marriages were often arranged. Connie Rust, a war bride, says of her Canadian soldier who had gone back to war, "I stayed behind

Note: All quotations are from *Blackouts to Bright Lights: Canadian War Bride Stories*, Barbara Ladouceur and Phyllis Spence, eds. Vancouver: Ronsdale Press, 1995.

and planned the wedding, never knowing if I would ever see him again. I planned it in five days." After the weddings, sometimes months later, more than forty thousand war brides, as they were known, prepared to move to Canada with the men they loved, leaving behind their lives in the U.K.

Granny told me a little about the Canadians she remembered, and I'd heard the phrase *war brides*, but I never considered it. What relevance did any of that have to my life, after all?

I was happily single. I owned my own flat in Manchester, north England, and I ran a little bookshop that sold second-hand books. I'd designed the interior of the shop myself, so it felt like an extension of my tiny apartment. Every morning, I checked the mail, switched on the computer, and worked on the novel I was writing for a couple of hours. Every afternoon, I listened to the drama production on Radio Four, scowling at any customer who needed assistance before it had finished. I knew lots of people in Manchester, so I went out most nights, returning home late for a brief sleep before going to work again.

Then, I took a weekend off to volunteer at the Cheltenham Literature Festival. I liked to hear "real" writers talking about their books because I wanted to be one myself someday. *That* was my life plan. To write novels. During the weekend in Cheltenham, I met a Canadian. He was friendly, interested in the world. I liked him. A lot.

I bumped into him again in Manchester two months later, and we went for dinner. Three weeks after that, I went to see him in Frankfurt for a weekend. A big jump from dinner to a weekend away, especially as we hadn't seen each other in the meantime. He thought I was sweet, bright, and generous. I thought he was kind, sweet, and clever. Seems with those six adjectives, well, five if you remember we both used *sweet*, our lives were about to change.

After Frankfurt—a glorious, heady time—I was realistic about the fact that we'd probably never see each other again. But then he emailed and told me I'd slipped into his heart like a spy. He called every day. We had lots to talk about. He invited me to Vancouver to meet him for a holiday. I agreed to go. That was the first time he asked me to come and live with him in Saskatoon. He had a nine-month work commitment there starting in the fall. I didn't answer.

A month after our weekend in Frankfurt, my plane flew into Vancouver. I looked down through the clouds at the gorgeous stretch of ocean bordering the mountains, at the glassy skyscrapers, the wide streets, and realized I knew nothing about the country where I was about to land. I'd been so caught up in our romance that I hadn't thought to look at a map, to read a guidebook, to consider any facts about Canada. Yann stood holding flowers in the airport. Shyly, we kissed. On our bed, Yann had carefully laid out lots of presents, all wrapped in red tissue paper. Each one had something to do with Canada: a tiny wooden canoe, a book of Canadian trivia, a doll wearing a Canadian flag, a toy moose in a tin can.... He asked me, again, if I'd like to move to Saskatoon. I was too tired to think, let alone reply, and I fell into a restless, jet-lagged sleep.

Three days after I arrived in Vancouver, as we hiked together in the mountains around Squamish, he told me he loved me. I'd been hoping he'd say it first—the words *I love you, I love you, I love you* had been at the tip of my tongue since we'd kissed at Vancouver airport. Since, perhaps, the first time we met.

We started a road trip to Saskatoon to see the house he'd found, he said, for us. Even though I hadn't said yes to living with him yet, I thought the drive would be fun. The idea of actually moving to Canada hadn't seemed real when he'd asked before. Now, with the tissue paper–wrapped presents and the road trip and the *I love you*'s, it seemed a little more possible, a little more real. So we got in the car and headed east.

Saskatchewan is a vast, gently undulating place. Everyone thinks it's flat, but it's not. The long, straight roads cut through an emptiness full of subtle changes. Every road is populated with tiny towns, some emptied of their inhabitants and filled with houses rotting as the years go by, some full of life and ambition, full of the future.

Driving on, we made out faint skyscrapers jutting into the huge sky. This was my welcome to Saskatoon. As we got closer, we could see the skyscrapers were squat and fairly ugly. We drove along hideous roads filled with big-box stores and headed downtown. We passed streets lined with clapboard houses, each dwelling different from the next, and crossed the river, the South Saskatchewan, glittery as it slowly rolled by that summer day.

I noticed the city, but mainly I noticed that the more days I spent with the man in the car next to me, the harder it was going to be to leave him. We laughed together, listened to bad music, argued, got lost. Until, finally, we turned the corner into the wide, tree-lined street where the new house was, and parked.

We walked into the pretty yellow rental, looked at the rooms empty of furniture, climbed the stairs to the bare bedroom with wooden floors and a view. "This can be your office," he said. And suddenly the possible future dawned on me, and I was scared. I started to cry.

"It'll be okay," he said. "It's only for nine months."

"I haven't said yes, yet."

He smiled, we cuddled, we got back in the car and went for supper, went to the cinema, already one of our favourite things to do. I asked myself while watching the movie, *How could I not live with this man?* I could hardly bear to be apart from him.

Many of the war brides didn't think in depth about their impending move to Canada—the war was on. Connie Rust, the woman who planned her wedding in five days, horrified her mother because, she explains, "I had only mentioned his name once to her in a letter saying I had been out with him, and then I phoned her up and asked her to come to my wedding next Saturday."

I love the stories of these rapid romances, similar yet so different from my own story. My favourite war bride is Margaret Brown, who says of the soldier she'd met five days before, "... and he said to me, 'Let's get married.' I got the giggles so much I couldn't stop laughing and I said, 'I don't even know you, Bob, never mind marry you.'" But they did get married, and she moved to Vancouver.

Back in my flat in Manchester, I wanted to make a decision. I missed Yann so badly, I hated it. He'd phone in the middle of the night, never quite grasping the time difference, and tell me he missed me too. He talked as if it was already decided that I'd move to Saskatoon, and perhaps, in a way, it was. I shut the door, switched off my phone, and considered my options. I lay on the bed and closed my eyes. I couldn't see how my relationship could survive the huge distance—I had friends who'd tried long-distance love, and it was hard. Added to that, Yann and I hardly knew each other; we'd spent, in total, less than four weeks actually together. How long could we sustain a relationship with only that to go on? I opened my eyes and looked round at my home, a flat I loved and had owned for only a year. Oh God, I already knew I couldn't be apart from him for months on end. I was moving to Canada and that was that.

When I was fourteen, I used to lie on the floor of my room in London. I'd have loud, terrible music playing—I've always had bad taste in music, with a tendency to replay one beloved song over and over, driving whoever else was in the house mad. The sky beyond my window filled with my dreams for my future. Between the clouds, because there are forever clouds in the sky in the U.K., I imagined who I wanted to be, where I wanted to live, and whom I was going to marry. I'd read far too many romance novels, smuggled to me by my Dutch grandmother, and so I had a specific hero in mind.

He was dark and tall, of course. He was a little older, but not much. He had curly hair. And he spoke three languages. In order for him to be so multilingual, I randomly decided he'd be Brazilian. I'd move to Brazil, leaving the wet and hopeless shores of miserable England far behind. My family, who tormented me simply by existing, would get the odd postcard from the beach where my man and I had set up a backpacker hostel. Our wedding would happen on the white sand: me, barefoot, wearing a simple dress, a string of tropical flowers in my hair.

I lay there, listening to music, imagining this future, loving the man who must be looking up at the same sky as me from his vantage point in Brazil, his arms folded so his hands rested behind his head.

And now, ten years later, I was about to pack everything in and move for love. So Yann wasn't Brazilian, but he did happen to speak three languages. And he had dark, curly hair.

At the end of the war, mainly in 1946, the war brides were gathered up and brought to Canada in specially commissioned ships, where they chatted together on the roiling oceans about the mysterious futures they would have on Canadian shores with their husbands, some of whom they hadn't seen since the wedding.

But I had nothing in common with them. I hadn't lived during a war, I hadn't had to move to a town I'd never seen before (I'd spent a whole night in Saskatoon during the summer), and I didn't have to travel for three weeks to get to the love of my life—I could just jump on a plane and fly through the northern lights–filled air. I had email and the phone to get in touch with people at home. I could leave any time I wanted. Moving was going to be easy, Canada was going to be easy—it was only for nine months. The war brides, so different from me, often left the U.K., not to return for years. They arrived, stepping into the arms of men who were practically strangers, and launched their new lives. Yet, despite the differences, four years after arriving in Saskatoon, I happened to go to a war brides exhibition. The walls were lined with planks of wood, each detailed with a photograph of a war bride. Playing on the speakers were the voices of some of the women. I sat and listened. Suddenly, an hour had gone by, then two. I couldn't stop listening to the stories, even when the tape looped back to the beginning and played again. In the same way that I listen to music, playing the same song over and over, I found myself fervently attending to these stories of homesickness, of love, of fear, of misery and great happiness. Tears filled my eyes. I felt as though I understood a tiny bit what it might have been like. I thought they might understand how *I* felt living so far from my family, from my home.

Notice, *four years*, not nine months. And now it's six. Yann instantly fell in love with Saskatoon; he was possibly as infatuated with the place as he was with me. He loved the wide skies, the sense of community, the feeling of belonging. And I loved him. After nine months, he hadn't wanted to leave. So we stayed.

Sitting in the war brides exhibition, listening to the audio recording of women describing the terrible homesickness, the aching sense of loss, the rip through the heart of belonging nowhere, emotions all bracketed by their funny stories of the freezing winters and silly language mistakes, I heard in their words something I recognized. Because I hadn't found moving to Canada easy. Not at all.

At first, I was too wrapped up in Yann to really notice all I'd left behind. But as time went by, it became apparent that I missed home. I know when I was fourteen, I'd fantasized about living on a beach in Brazil. But now that fantasy seemed wrong to me. I didn't want to live on a beach in Brazil. I didn't want to live in Saskatoon. I wanted to live just down the road from my mum, in London. I wanted to be able to see my family every few days, to hang out with the friends I was losing touch with. But Yann didn't want to move back to Britain—funnily enough, he found the weather damp. And, although I find Canada far harder than I'd imagined, I don't want to leave him. One of the war brides, Margaret Presley, says, "Everything that's different sort of hits you." Lots of things are different about Canada, about Saskatoon. I didn't notice at first, but as the years have gone by I can't help but realize that the insane winters, when there's snow on the ground for months of the year, are hard on me. Endlessly, I make cultural mistakes, such as the time I went to a potluck empty-handed and the tables groaned with food the other guests had brought. Or the time my unknown neighbour kindly brought me pasta sauce and I looked at her as though she were mad at best, a serial killer at worst.

When I say *pavement* or *autumn* or *post* or *purse* or *jumper* to a person from Saskatchewan, I get a puzzled look or a smile of wry amusement. And at least five times a week, someone sweetly tells me about a visit to some remote part of England or a great-aunt who lives somewhere in the outskirts of London.

As time went by and I managed to notice a world outside Yann, the little differences made me more homesick. Homesickness is a curse—it's physically painful, a deep wrenching in the stomach. And it makes no sense, it has no root in reason, because Saskatoon is one of the most perfect places I've ever been. The size of the community suits me well, the people are kind and open, the cultural life is varied and accessible, the weather, although brutal, is fodder for the imagination. The empty space gives me room to write. All these things are crucial for my day-to-day life. But they don't stop me from missing home.

I miss silly things: drinking cups of tea, reading the *Guardian*, listening to Radio Four—all things easily replicated in Saskatoon, but somehow not quite the same. When the air glitters in the middle of winter, I long for rain; when I hear a British accent, I want to run over to the person speaking and give him or her a hug. I've been startled by an intensity of longing for things I took for granted in the U.K.—sitting in the garden with my mother, listening to my granny tell a story, exchanging banter with people in the shops.

Unlike the war brides, I get to go back to the U.K. fairly often. And for the first couple of years, nothing was hugely changed by my emigration. Things with my friends were pretty much the same, things with my family similar to how they had been before. But then, over the years, distances began to open up between me and my friends, because while I was off living my new life, they'd gone ahead and got on with theirs. They weren't waiting for me to drop back home; they weren't wondering what I was up to, not really, not anymore. I've had to accept that most of them won't, can't, be part of my life anymore. Although it's hard to say goodbye, and I've found it terribly difficult to let go, it's worse trying to hold on to something that has gone.

I listened to the war brides talking about the people they'd left behind. They didn't have email, phones, and now Facebook to help them cope with the long distances. When they said goodbye, it meant goodbye. Yet they seemed to cope. I wonder if part of the modern immigrant's dilemma is that we can easily stay in touch with people back home. Perhaps it makes it harder to cut off, to let go, to say goodbye when we can just pick up the phone. And I've had to learn that even though I'm still in touch with people "back home," I do have to say goodbye. I have to leave and let go. Hard as it is with my friends, it's much, much harder with my family. I miss my sister and brother, my mum and dad, and all the other family members whom, when I was fourteen and fantasizing about Brazil, I thought I could live without. My granny turns ninety-five this fall, but I can't go to her birthday because I have to be in Saskatoon. I have a life here now. Either the war brides were more stoic than I am, or today's modern communication conveniences leave me in neither place. Sometimes I feel fully nowhere, unlike the war brides who had to make a complete break. Instant travel and Skype give me access to all I've left behind, but I am left with part of me clinging on to that past, much as I know I have to move forward to the future.

The war brides were braver than me; they dealt with greater hardships. Sure, Saskatoon is cold in winter, but *imagine* it without central heating. That's how some of them had to live.

Sure, it's hard meeting new people in a new community, but some of the war brides were ostracized for "stealing" the Canadian men. And yes, there are differences between Canada and the U.K., but the differences are less extreme for me than they were for them. The war brides talk about wooden sidewalks and outhouses, or living with no electricity on the Prairies when they first arrived. A war bride, Betty Patriquin, says this about moving to Canada, and it sticks with me when I feel homesick:

> *You put out of your mind how sad you are about leaving your family.... You're very torn, and I think with all the war brides this has been a common dilemma. Some of them settled down in Canada immediately and never worried about England again. Others never really adjusted to coming here. They'll always have one foot in England and one foot here.*

That's how I feel—as though I have one foot in each country. But when I think I can't bear that feeling, when I am frustrated with my own homesickness, I'll settle down and read one of the stories of the war brides and feel soothed.

The relationship with Yann continues to go well. We've started a family and bought a house near a fun street in Saskatoon where there's a cinema and pleasant cafés. The house is painted in all the colours we love, bright orange and yellow, and it has wooden floors, just like the house he showed me years ago where I cried and he reassured me. Some of the things that were once important to me are still very much part of my life—I'm a writer now and that's what I always wanted.

Sometimes, I still get sad, living so far from my family, from the country I still think of as my home. When I get too homesick I think of all those who came before me. Those brave British women who just got on with it. That's, perhaps, what I need to learn to do. Together, my dark-curly-haired, trilingual Canadian and I are making a new home. We're weaving our story into Canada, a land full of people who have moved or have been moved, a place open to those of us who are ready to let go of our old lives and embrace a future of unknown possibility, just as the war brides did. Although I couldn't have predicted it, falling in love with a Canadian is slowly teaching me to fall in love with Canada.

A Caravan
of Words

RACHEL MANLEY

My cat got into Canada before I could.

In 1986 it coasted through immigration at Mirabel airport in
Montreal without a hitch. All it needed was the inoculations and
a cat kennel required by Air Canada. I first met the scrawny,
injured tabby at a Canadian diplomat's home in Barbados. It
was on its way to the local pound that very evening. I secretly
decided to keep it, for deep in my heart I felt that a Barbadian
puss shouldn't meet its end through foreign edict. So I offered
to take it to the pound for them. I called the kitten Freda. In
time, it became clear that she was a he. So Freda became Fred
and settled into the family.

I, unlike Fred, had to wait several months to be allowed into
Canada. I had married a Canadian who lived in Montreal, and I
applied from Barbados where I worked to join him under family
reunification. The move wasn't straightforward. Although
Fred's name change didn't seem to matter to the Canadians, I
first had to change my married surname legally back to its
maiden status of Manley to conform to the Napoleonic Code of
ancient French law used in Quebec. It was a sign of things to

come. Linguistic estrangement, more than anything else, would make this passage my exile.

I was homesick even before I landed at Mirabel airport. Knowing that only French was spoken in this province made it seem even more foreign to me than its snow did. I was reminded of how I had felt at age eleven going for the first time to boarding school far away in the bauxite-red hills of rural Jamaica. There, I would wake up every morning to my sadness. But I had a Scottish teacher who explained that if I treated my mind as my home, and my thoughts as my company, I would never feel homesick wherever I roamed. "Make it your caravan," she said in her mellifluous brogue.

So now each morning in Montreal, as soon as I woke, I'd fight the urge to cry and seek once more the company of my thoughts in the safety of what I've come to believe is my mobile home. In there I'd find those waking thoughts that realign themselves like drifting clouds, the mind preparing to reconnect us to the world after the solitude of sleep—thoughts that could make a home of Kingston and Mandeville, Jamaica, or of England, Africa, Barbados, and Canada. First homes or last ones. Home is the mind. As if holding on to a dream, I imagined I was still in the Caribbean and would wake to a world that was warm, its landscape and people familiar. How do we think before we can speak? Thoughts come from anywhere, from any place and any time; they arrive on words, and I'd take those words when I woke and write simple poems, as though putting myself on record, as slowly each truth would return, one by one, like a count of last night's sheep.

Canada is stubborn about rights: one's right to one's health and education, social security, and language. It is a country whose personality is otherwise quite without chauvinism, which may be why some people call it bland. Canada is a rare instance of official bilingualism in the New World. English and French cohabit, though not always comfortably. Who knows if this bilingualism resulted in a national value of language, but nearly a century and a half after this country was established, the international issue of Newsweek magazine rated Canada as the top country to live in as a fiction writer. Reading this would remind me that histories are longer than migrations, and that our own Caribbean story really begins in the Garden of Eden, not at the point of European arrival at Jamaica's Columbus Cove.

As a Jamaican, I come from a region where each island holds on to its own unique character. The official language of Jamaica is English. It has replaced hundreds of small, imported tribal African tongues, whose mute echoes are now no more than the rhythm of our music or a distant yearning for meaning we can never quite conjure up. When I was a child, anyone with an education was expected to speak perfectly enunciated, uncorrupted standard English, to doggedly resist dropping an *h* or putting one in the wrong place. (Actually, the slaves didn't learn the language "improperly," as the English thought—they learned it well enough to mispronounce it cleverly so that their masters couldn't understand them. Derek Walcott and V.S. Naipaul would eventually prove that not only in cricket could we beat our masters at their own game!) But nowadays it's fashionable—and, in fact, viewed by many as nationalistic—to speak the more commonly heard Jamaican dialect known as *patois* or the modern Rastafarian I-and-I talk of peace-pipe spiritual love. It is proof that one is Jamaican and "rootsy."

As a child of mixed bloods, the colonizers and the colonized, I am a hybrid of different sorrows, and English, in all its evil and its good, is part of me. Whether I like it or not. I was educated in schools where my teachers were often English or "well-spoken" Jamaicans. I was never academically inclined, and I studied English at university only because I have always loved to write. Apart from dutifully learned declensions in Latin and Spanish, now forgotten, I spoke only English. Arriving in Canada, I had thought of myself as a poet. But most importantly, all my life language had been my subject, my currency, my consolation and refuge, my inlet and outlet. I was adrift without it. Now faced with this exotic, melodic, acrobatic French tongue, I felt mute and totally paralyzed by incomprehension. I was unable to understand a word of the sounds around me—I might as well have been in Paris or Guadeloupe; in the dark, I couldn't tell the difference.

In addition to the language, I was bewildered by this province that was angry with its federation, which had only marginally survived a referendum to separate Quebec from English Canada. Here I was, an anglophone, in a French underdog province, a position unnatural for me. It felt as though I lay on the wrong side of history. I came from a family who believed in Caribbean federation, an instinct forged from our island's common past. This was quite different. Here, federalism was threatened by two very unlike and often competitive European traditions whose countries had fought for the acquisition of Canada, and one had been defeated. I figured that at least in the Caribbean we were all united in kicking out the British.

Montreal is elegantly green and unafraid of sentimental ornamentation, with wide-shouldered, robust buildings and parks that brave the slopes of their central mountain. We had moved to Outremont, a largely middle-class area on the side of Mount Royal, away from downtown. Our home was the large, airy, top-floor flat of a duplex that was always collecting some angle of sunshine, even on the bleakest winter day. We were taking over a lease from a painter who loved its light.

Two separate duplexes sat side by side, with four flats: two up and two down. The tenancy of this complex reflected the conundrum that is Canada. The upstairs flats were linked visually at the front by matching balconies and at the rear by small iron fire escapes beyond the kitchens. The next-door upper flat was home to a very tall family we fondly called the Trees, except for the matriarch, a comparatively small Italian lady of indulgent heart who worked at an old people's home and would return after intermittent deaths to the tiny rear balcony, where I'd see her sitting, quietly weeping. Her husband was an American commercial filmmaker. Their two six-foot daughters were what most young Montrealers are today—multilingual, speaking English, French, and, in this case, Italian.

Beneath us lived the Joyal family, and beside them, Madam Joyal's parents, the Tremblays, who owned the complex. After several weeks of trying to greet the obdurate, wordless neighbours below where we shared an entrance hall, I left a bag of Jamaican Blue Mountain coffee with an introductory note. The coveted beans enchanted not even a smile from them. He would nod without looking at me, and Madame simply held her pretty head down and swished past me like an eel in water disappearing into the shadows of her sanctum. So strange, I thought, coming from islands where culture, size, proximity, and temperament make neighbours of us all. These people have no "broughtupsy," I concluded, resorting to a good Jamaican word.

"Perhaps they don't speak English," I suggested to Juliana next door.

"How you mean they no speak Engaleesh!" She declared more than asked the question with her energetic Italian inflection. "They met at Harvard University! No, they *won't* speak Engaleesh."

Meanwhile, we had taken in another stray, a sleek black female cat, as company for Fred. We called her Freda. Once again, Fred acclimatized immediately, communicating in whatever language Quebecois cats meow or purr in, striking up a loving friendship with his feline counterpart.

I, however, couldn't get a decent job or speak to a neighbour, and, even if I could be understood, was in a place I couldn't understand. I was very jealous of this world of my husband, with its fashionable French women and the exotic language he was fluent in, from which I felt excluded. In Montreal, most of the theatres played current English movies, so we'd go out to a film and dinner. In a steak house strewn with sawdust, reminiscent of Jamaican dairies, we sat opposite each other at a rustic bench. My husband was facing the door. I drank wine and watched him drink his beer. He could see the door, and suddenly he brightened and waved.

"Allô, Michel," he called out.

I waited for my steak, aware that his gaze had followed this Michelle person, checking now and then to make sure she was still there. An old girlfriend, I decided, or maybe a present one. When the steak arrived, charred and yet juicing, on a blatantly unpretentious tin plate, I announced a headache.

"I want to go home," I said.

My husband gamely called for the bill, and I enjoyed his unspoken regret. Did he think I was going to sit there while he ogled Michelle?

As we were leaving, he waved to a man I could now see seated at a far table.

"Salut, Michel."

Michel, he now explained, was an announcer from work.

A male announcer.

The gender subtleties of French and its pronunciation were lost on me. Defeated by language again.

Since I couldn't purr or yeowl, I decided I'd better learn French. I joined an extension class at a local university and tried diligently with my teacher, a Monsieur Beauchamp. It was by now the January term, and I had hunkered down, making my warm flat home, seldom going outdoors—the winter of 1986 was said to be fierce, but what did I know? It was a world I could not have imagined possible. Mountains of snow that before had been no more than pictures on Christmas cards we'd received while on holiday by the sea in Ocho Rios. White can be so pretty on its own, glamorous and silly. I was used to it in lace or the cotton sheets at home, which always smelled of dry khus khus grass or mothballs. White was almost like its own colour in summer: frivolous in June roses, elegant in orchids. Blank white lime-washed walls and the base of trees, white that so easily showed dirt or a mark or a stain; white pants beware a panty line; white swimsuits that looked sheer when wet. Now this whiteness of snow, monumental and silent. The thing I noticed first was that snow has no smell at all. It seemed meaningless to me heaped over everything like packaging for some journey. I decided to flop down backwards in my bulky, loud yellow duvet coat to make a snow angel. My husband helped me up and explained about dog pee or worse trapped beneath. For me, not even the snow was understood.

But from my window, winter was not all that daunting. I have never been adventurous or athletic. I hate outdoors and picnics, day trips and sightseeing. As a teenager I loved rainy weekends when my sporty friends couldn't get to the beach to tan or water ski. I am the original killjoy, the mean indoor spirit that likes to know it's not missing out on anything. So winter's inadvertent malevolence suited me, and the cats and I watched it from the safety of our windows.

I bought French immersion tapes and listened to them at night, sometimes falling asleep to the strange sounds my mind unwittingly absorbed. I'd wake with some small exchange stuck in my head.

"Où est la clé?"

"La clé est ici."

But if I'd found the key, it wasn't opening any doors for me.

I got extra help from the taller of the Tree sisters next door, whose face flushed each time she failed to convey the concept of how to make a French verb negative.

"Vous allez à New York?" she'd ask again patiently.

And I never could figure out whether I je ne pas visite, or I je ne visite pas, or quite what it was I or Messieurs Mercier or Durand in my study book did with theirs either.

"Où est la chat?" asked the Tree.

"C'est mon chat. Mon chat est Fred." I tried to remember what "où est" meant. "Mon dieu!" I declared in a phrase I did know. The cat had escaped.

Fred returned days later, bringing many new friends with him: ticks, fleas, and mange.

Finally, in my tenth week, Monsieur Beauchamp, who despaired of my ability to pronounce his sensual vowels, threw down his book on the desk in front of him.

"Madame Manley, you are *murdering* my language," he declared, sounding like an anguished Maurice Chevalier.

I stood waiting for the number 129 bus in minus-twenty weather, too frozen to cry or laugh, my eyes dry with cold, my nose hurting. I was utterly mute. The cars, as they passed me, seemed to reflect my dilemma on their licence plates: "Je me souviens." I could never forget my past either. I took refuge in the certainty that sooner or later I'd get back home....

I felt sure there was no place for me in Canada. My electric typewriter provided the only comfort. I found myself needing more room than the poetic frame, lengthening my sentences, explaining my thoughts long-windedly over and over to myself or to the page, eking out breath in an effort to be heard, Fred, unperturbed, asleep at my feet.

My despairing husband persuaded his friendly physician to try hypnosis on me.

"You *vary*, *vary* tired, eyes they *vary* heavy."

Now, how was I to be hypnotized when instead I was mentally correcting his English, inserting verbs and definite articles?

Finally, defeated, my husband arranged a transfer to Toronto. We packed up two lifetimes of books and my Jamaican paintings, and I left without sentimental farewell.

In anglophone Ontario I discovered my Canada. At last I was able to speak to people who would listen to me and answer, hear me and understand. Even the annoying invasion of telemarketing calls was now welcome. They spoke in English. They spoke a milder version of American—still a twang, but a less-shrill defiance of English reserve.

They say that if the United States is a melting pot of cultures, then Canada is a mosaic. This is doubly true of Toronto. And language is the outline setting each culture apart. The brush-stroke hieroglyphics of Chinatown mark the windows in black and red along Spadina. The round patterns of Russian along Bathurst and Steeles; the linear lashes and dashes, a scripted flowing hemstitch of Arabic in Mississauga. Each wave of immigrant has their own street festival, their national costumes, their food, their instruments, their sorrow. Yet, against the threat of U.S. cultural imperialism, Canada often defines itself by what it is not, giving its neighbour more than a simply proverbial cold shoulder.

In the past, I would return from England or the United States with clothes and shoes, memories of fine theatre, and stories of sights I'd seen in my brief escape. But now, as a migrant, I felt like a traitor. Here I was in the First World, soothing my conscience with placebos: I had married a foreigner whose work was here, in his country—what else could I do? But deep inside I knew I came from a region that had educated me, shaped me in every way from its limited resources, and I had left without giving anything back. I was filled with guilt.

I holed up in my townhouse at my desk in front of a window framing a maple tree whose seasons I would come to know leaf by leaf, bough by bough, as the neighbours changed in the windows beyond. At my new computer I was evoking my past, telling my story. In brief forays, I would brave the city for necessities. My health card, my bank, my weekly trip to the supermarket, the post office, or the pharmacy. After the gracious avenues of Montreal, with its sidewalk cafés and residents—even the beggars—whose avant-garde demeanour, their dress, how they walked and talked, and how they arranged themselves seemed almost artistic, Toronto seemed somehow narrower and more focused, less dissipated in passion and calamity; its roads seemed about direction, its citizenry bent toward purpose, their dress unimportant; its panhandlers scruffy and direct in their approach. Or maybe the difference was simply that now I understood what people were saying.

But whether Montreal or Toronto, this was the land of Margaret Laurence and Mordecai Richler, Margaret Atwood and Robertson Davies. It was also the land of Austin Clarke and Dionne Brand, Cecil Foster and Olive Senior. This was the land of Canada Council for the Arts, of arts grants and prizes. It was a First World nation that had turned its heart to literature. It cared that its people read books. It cared that they wrote them in either language.

It would take time, but as a Jamaican Canadian, a citizen of both countries, I would move from my own underbrush of poetry to lawns of prose. And back in my language, I found it easier to settle in and write that prose, now that I had a potential audience. Here, I could unburden myself of my guilt by writing another piece of Jamaica's story. My estrangement from both the past and the present slowly became the pages of a book.

And so, ten years after landing in Canada, and four years after coming to Toronto, I was published. Not exactly an overnight triumph, but I'll say it for Canada: a story of my island and its brief two years within a federation, and the memories of ancestors who had made a difference to that cause, held worth for this country's readers. I got grants from the Canada Council, and I even won a Governor General's Award with not a single mention of Canada in my story.

But you know, there is always one pivotal moment when things become real, be it a story, a country, a person, a relationship, or a place. When what is only a set of dancing ideas suddenly pulls together and makes sense. That moment came for me soon after I arrived in Toronto.

"Yes, Rachel speaking."

"Oh hello. I am calling from the immigration court. We need a translator."

"Oh?" I was mystified.

"We understand you speak Ah-da ...?"

"Ah-da?" I wondered if this was a joke being played on me by someone who knew I'd long needed a job, so long, in fact, I'd given up trying to find one.

"The Jamaican language?"

"Why?" I asked.

"A Jamaican refugee has requested an interpreter, and by law we must provide one. You were suggested."

Unseen, I rolled my eyes. A Jamaican refugee from what? I saw through the scam.

"We pay seventy-five dollars an hour—even if the case isn't heard that day, once you attend court, we will pay you a minimum of four hours."

I thought about this. It made no sense. As a graduate of English at our university, I knew of no language called Ah-da. But I also knew there was no Jamaican I couldn't understand, translate for, or explain to, and I needed the money.

"Okay," I said. "Let me know when."

A Jamaican friend phoned to ask if I'd received the call. She had given my name.

"But what is Ah-da?" I asked, looking at Fred, who had wandered in as though to take the call. Being a Barbadian cat, he didn't care at all.

"Don't be ridiculous! How you going to interpret Jamaican if you don't know that?"

I was confused. Indeed, I had signed on for a language whose very name eluded me.

"When they asked the man if he spoke English, he must have said no, he spoke the ah-da language."

"Oh, the *other!*"

Obvious, indeed.

It seems a small thing. In fact, I went only once; the case was postponed, and I never was called to the courts on College Street again. But in the Canadian context, I had found my small place. I still receive the occasional package of guidelines. I believe I'm still the official Jamaican interpreter. A small tile in the Canadian mosaic, I've found my place as a group member and seen my country represented with my mastery over language, even the one they called Ah-da.

It seems all my life every important concept has come down to language. Slaves, words. Montreal, words. Exile, words. Toronto, words.

Was Canada my country now? Was Jamaica? Was England the land of my language and my other heritage?

More words.

My mind is my home; thoughts are my companions. I lure them out from an alphabet of possibility. I live in a caravan of words.

Under the
Armpit of Noah

BOONAA MOHAMMED

"Get up you little baby."
Some kids chuckled, others remained silent,
and still others didn't know what to think.
He tried his best to ignore them,
still unsure of many things,
but knew he was standing face to face
with his worst nightmare.

A tall, curly-headed Jewish kid named Noah.
A tight red winter jacket covering the anger he wore
underneath. Big for his age.
Way too big for his age,
with a purple scarf wrapped loosely around his neck
dangling behind his left leg.

In his dreams he wished to have the pleasure of humiliating
Noah in a similar fashion or worse,
once a week or on a daily basis.
At night time when no one was around

and only God was there to listen,
he prayed that he would come to school the next day to hear
the tragic news of Noah's demise.
Family burned alive or some other horrible set of tragic events
to mimic the desperate feeling of unhappiness
that he slept with
tucked away
under his pee-drenched mattress.

"What are you some kind of faggot?"

He responded with a winded, "No."

"Do you miss your mommy?"
The small group of children surrounding them began to laugh.

"Well, do you?"

"NO!" He gasped for breath, trying to swallow whatever bit of
frigid oxygen he could get;
his heart was pounding 304 miles per second,
trying just to stay alive and not show anyone that inside he had
already begun to cry,
but by this point he could feel a tiny tingle in his cheekbone
and the cold wind made boogers flow down his nose like the
Nile,
only a few minutes had passed but the smell of tension made
him feel like they had been there forever.

"I bet you want your monkey mommy to come and feed you
milk from her boobies; is that what you want?"

The kids began to laugh hysterically and other kids on the
playground took notice and also began to crowd,
the small crowd became a mini-mob,
the mentality of which made everyone crave blood,
little vampires sucking down the juice of disgruntled
innocence.

Every playground kingdom deserves a King and here he was,
King Noah
armed with everything a little boy could ever want,
power,
fear,
respect and attention from those who attention seek'd not.

"Come here little monkey, let Mommy feed you."
At that instant he pulled the little boy by his toque,
introducing his neck to whiplash,
forcing his fragile head against his chest,
all the other kids began to laugh,
for this was the show,
this was what they all came to see,
the live execution of the one who did not look like thee.

The tingle became tingling
turning into heavy breathing;
pacing
vibrating
his heart began bleeding from all the beating it was receiving.

"Does that taste good little monkey? I bet you like to suck on
your mommy's boobies don't you little monkey?"

This was officially the funniest thing
most of these kids had ever seen.
The choke hold was getting tight,
the little boy could barely breathe
but the laughter was too much,
Noah just could not stop, his crowd demanded more,
they roared while he scored, intoxicated off support,
he swore to give them more, more and more
feeding off the energy from the crowd
made him squeeze the head a little tighter until
things became blurry,
people would not stop moving,
the sky became the ground,
the ground would not stop moving,
there were so many of them,
all of them would not stop moving,
no matter how much he yelled or pushed or screamed or fought
he couldn't seem to get out of it,
so he gave up,
tired of fighting,
he surrendered his free will, for this was his destiny,
to be enslaved under the armpit of Noah.

The faint white light helped him think.
Amongst the madness of schoolyard adolescence he had an
unforgiving moment of clarity.
Finally a time to reflect,
and he suddenly remembered how he had got there.

It all started the previous year when he found out he looked
like a monkey on account of his black skin.

A class trip to the zoo and Noah pointed out the resemblance
between the two, one hung from trees, the other hung out after
school.
Monkey
was one of the nicer names he would have gotten called,
bad names at that age,
these kids knew them all.

He would come home sore,
his back hurt from all the stabbing and biting.
If it was up to him his name would have been
Christopher or Michael,
but instead he got a funny African name
that nobody could even pronounce,
he blamed his parents
thought maybe they didn't care for him enough,
why else would they set him up to be the butt of every joke,
he joked about changing his name
but his parents never listened,
thought he was a little strange,
but the strange thing is that he had internalized he was
different,
and at that age who wants to be different,
he would have preferred to be like his friends
a quarter Irish, Scottish, Welsh and English.

He would trade his nappy hair for approval if they let him,
remove his parents' accents and replace them with acceptance.

And most of all he wanted everyone to stop asking him where
he was from.

He still wasn't sure what they meant,
he was born in a hospital down the road,
he thought he was from here.

It was not the first time he had dealt with this terrorist,
in fact recently it seemed like it was becoming a regular affair,
although usually he got lucky and a teacher would interfere.
Today the cold weather was severe and led the children
behind one of the portables to play a traditional
schoolyard game of Red Rover.
The game was usually only played during lunch because recess
was usually done by the time they got their snow pants on.
They played other games like ledgers,
cops and robbers and rocket ball which was just American
football with a tennis ball using standard Canadian Football
League rules including four downs and absolutely no girls.
As a microcosm of society,
the playground consisted of a loose hierarchy based on class,
race and gender.

He had more strikes against him than in his favour.

Daily he would tell himself he didn't care
about what other people thought,
because the people who cared didn't matter,
and the people who mattered
didn't care.

Although the barriers we build to keep out pain
can sometimes keep out joy as well,
he wanted friends so he did what they did and he did it well;
but on this particular day

the cold weather during the first weeks of December meant that
most of the teachers on duty that lunch were actually inside
watching from a window.
Unions had no cure for frostbite, so the kids congregated on
concrete with no authority in sight.

It was the Wild West where the fist was the law and the law
was always meant to be broken.
It was during a "friendly" game of Red Rover that our friend
Noah decided his masculinity had been called into question.
In order to preserve his honour and send a message to the
other alpha males,
it was important he make a statement
they would not forget.

The strategy in Red Rover is that when you get called over,
you try and destroy the weakest chain leaving the other side's
foundation barely intact.
The game in many ways is symbolic to the ways in which the
strongest people in society find the weakest and attack.
So Noah attacks the kid with the funny name and the world's
scrawniest frame and ironically the only one amongst them
who is Muslim and black.

He ties up his boots, one rabbit under each hole,
pulling the string back into a perfect bow.
He's pumped, eyes gazed, ready to rock locked on his target,
all systems are go,
the wind fires him like a rocket,
running and running, like the sun when it's rising,
slowly becoming bigger and bigger his figure is mesmerizing,
he prepares to make contact,

they have narrowed down where he might land, he leans
towards the left with nothing but fist in his hand,
he is coming closer,
he looks like he just might do it, but instead of running like a
train through his chain, he instead runs right through him.

Boom, target, hit.

As our friend lay there,
kids hawked around the remains of what could have been our
first Black Muslim President,
or Prime Minister,

if they ever figured out he was Canadian.

People gathered around to pay their last respects,
there was no way
he could have survived what they all saw happen.

The sound of his head smashing against the pavement released
a sonic boom, heard and felt by most in the vicinity.

In order to not seem as weak as he really was,
he tried his best to stand up but the shove had left him winded.
It was hard for him to stand up completely,
so instead he kind of just knelt down.
There were probably around 12 kids who were playing the
game and all of them immediately rushed over
to see the damage that had been done.

Noah sensed the tension in the air
and knew that another trip to the office might prevent him from

going away to the cottage that weekend.
He had no choice;
he had to silence any potential uprising that might lead to
propaganda and interfere with his reign of terror.

"Get up you little baby."
Some kids chuckled, others remained silent,
and still others didn't know what to think.

He tried his best to ignore them,
still unsure of many things but knew he was standing face to
face with his worst nightmare.

"What are you some kind of faggot?"

The winded boy responded with a quiet, "No."

"Well then do you miss your mommy?" The small group of
children surrounding them began to laugh, "Well, do you?"

"NO," he answered.

Noah thought by turning the whole situation into a big joke that
nobody would be able to report his brute force,
but by this point our bully was split between making sure he
didn't get in trouble
and showing his schoolmates that he was nobody to mess with,
he began actually noticing
the reactions from the kids around him and figured
that if everybody was laughing
then nobody could get mad at him.

Noah remembered his monkey joke from the zoo,
thought about all the good that might do.

"Come here little monkey, let big mama feed you."
Now he was caught in the spotlight, as more children gathered
around he felt like some sort of ring master taming a wild
animal for everyone's delight.
He pulled the little boy by his toque, a cheap dollar store hat
that said Canada on its flap,
the anxious grab introduced the boy's neck to whiplash,
forcing his fragile head against his chest while all the other
kids began to laugh.

Even the kids he considered to be tough
started to join in on the festivities,
Noah took that as a sign of appreciation for his actions and
began to squeeze tighter while ignoring the whimpering cries
from below.

He looked down and saw the tears falling on his elbow,
it made him want to do it more,
everyone was watching, way more than before,
he couldn't let go,
his ego wouldn't let him,
look at him go,
tighter and tighter
until the breaths couldn't go,
and his blood couldn't flow
and he couldn't see anymore,
everyone was moving,
people would not stop moving,
the sky became the ground,

the ground would not stop moving,
there were so many of them,
all of them would not stop moving,
no matter how much he yelled
or pushed
or screamed
or fought
he couldn't seem to get out of it, so he gave up,
tired of fighting, he surrendered his free will,
for this was his destiny,
to be enslaved under the armpit of Noah.

Mrs. Bernard finally showed up and Noah finally let go.

His victim lay on the ground, barely moving any bones.
He didn't want to look up.
He was afraid of what humiliation looked like.
He knew everybody was staring at him,
he could feel their gazes on the back of his head.
Mrs. Bernard tried to move his arm
to see if he was o.k.
but he just pushed her away and insisted on being alone.

The kids were still laughing,
he could hear the giggles,
more of them slowly began to arrive,
somebody kicked snow at him
but Mrs. Bernard didn't turn around in time.

He did want his mommy.
He wanted his mommy to grab them by their nice little blond
hairs and beat them like piñatas until they bled dollar bills.

He insisted nobody touch him.
The principal walked over and told him to get up,
but instead he just cried more.
He cried
and cried
and cried and
cried
until his eyes began to feel sore.
He fell asleep in his own filth.
Jacket soaked with liquid from his face.
Anybody that tried to move him
found the job extremely aggravating.
Eventually they all left to go back inside after lunch was done.
Mrs. Bernard stayed with him outside while the principal got
his parents on the phone.
They said he wasn't co-operating and requested they come and
pick him up,
he had got into a fight,
and the zero tolerance policy meant that he had done too much.
He just sat there crying, curled up in a little ball of pity.

He wondered how many snowflakes would fall before the pain
would go away.

The office was warm; his face was nearly dry and he had cried
absolutely all that he could cry.
His father was in the principal's office trying to understand
why he had been called,
the school requested a translator,
Noah was sitting across the hall.
He could see his face,
Noah could see him too.

He just wanted to be friends, why did Noah hate him?
Why did he have to make fun of him,
why did he have to make his life so hard,
until why became irrelevant and he wanted something tangible
to help heal his scars.
He saw a big shiny apple on the secretary's desk,
a red shiny paper weight holding papers down on a plate.

His face went blank, no expression or method to his madness.
He tied up his boots, one rabbit under each hole,
pulling the string back into a perfect bow.

He was pumped,
eyes gazed, ready to rock locked on his target,
all systems are go, the wind fired him like a rocket,
he grabbed the apple off the desk
and walked over to where Noah sat.
Walking and walking
his bright figure resembled the moon rising,
slowly covering all the light Noah could see.
Left foot after right,
Noah looked up at him walking over,
everyone was confused,
our friend looked possessed,
he was a man on a mission;
the secretary stood up, asked,
"What do you think you're doing?"

He didn't hear what she had said
and it didn't really matter because regardless
he wasn't actually sure himself.
He watched Noah smirk,

and begin to giggle as the secretary ran after him,
but it was too late
he was preparing to make contact,
he narrowed down where he might land,
he was coming closer,
he looked like he just might do it.

Boom, target, hit.

Blood gushed from Noah's face;
the metal apple dropped and rolled leaving a trail of DNA
everywhere it went.

No smile is more beautiful than the one that struggles through
tears and despite the rough patches I generally enjoyed those
years,
especially that day,
when everyone learned it's the quiet kids who do the crazy
things

and a righteous slave can always overthrow a brutal King.

What's in a Name?

MAHTAB NARSIMHAN

"Hello, this is Maht—, I mean Matty. May I help you?"

It took me a long time and a lot of effort to get that greeting right.

My husband, son, and I arrived in Canada on a cold day in April 1997. After a fifteen-hour non-stop flight from halfway around the world, I had lost all sense of time. All I knew was that after months of packing, planning, and agonizing, I had finally crossed the threshold into the unknown: Canada.

In the arrivals lounge, against the backdrop of a grey sky, a sea of faces confronted us. The only consolation was, they were not all the same colour.

My first glimpse of Toronto was framed by mounds of dirty snow standing tall on the sidewalk. Back home I had only seen ice or snow, always pure white, in a freezer. People bundled up to their eyeballs hurried through the sliding doors. White smoke poured out of the exhaust pipes of cars lined up at the curb and hung in the air for several seconds before dissipating, as if shredded by unseen fingers. Watching from behind a wall of glass, I wondered why it did that. The answer was to dawn on me swiftly and brutally.

My sister had immigrated to Canada a year earlier and was there to receive us, carrying an armful of assorted jackets. My parents were there too; they'd moved here two months before us. Ten minutes of hugging later, I shrugged into a jacket and, without buttoning it up, stepped into a sunny, spring morning in Toronto. The wind sliced through me with the precision of a newly sharpened knife, and my heart almost seized up with the agonizing chill. My sister's laughter echoing in my ears, I buttoned my jacket with numb fingers and drew the hood over my head. *Nothing* could have prepared me for this biting, piercing cold that clawed at my face, whooshed down my neck, and left me feeling as though I were standing in a freezer, naked. I had just left the warm shores of home for this? A chilling thought numbed me: if this was spring, what was winter like?

My sister lived in the East York area of Toronto, and we decided to make it home, too. To us immigrants, Thorncliffe was a small piece of the familiar we could cling to, bringing home to us here, so far away from India. I'd walk by the Indian store, and the whiff of samosas frying in hot oil would remind me of the streets of Bombay. Children would be chattering rapidly to each other in Gujarati or Hindi, and instantly I'd be eavesdropping without meaning to. Someone wearing a shalwar-kurta would run past, a brilliant smear of red across a bleak landscape just recovering from a harsh winter. I would be reminded of Holi, the festival of colours just past.

Nostalgia would bubble up inside me, unbidden.

Out of habit, as if I were on an extended holiday, I converted the price of everything into Indian rupees. Though I had spent almost a year and a half in the Middle East, home was still

Bombay (Mumbai). It took forty Indian rupees to buy a Canadian dollar, and that was my yardstick for measuring the cost of living.

A bunch of coriander cost forty rupees? I decided that I really didn't need coriander in my food. Not till I got a job, anyway! A cup of tea cost fifty rupees? I very rarely treated myself to a coffee or tea outside. I agonized over every purchase, big or small. Should I buy that iron? Or vacuum cleaner? Would I be here long enough to *really* use it?

After many months, I finally stopped converting. On that day I decided not to look back. *This* was our present and future. My son loved Toronto, and after celebrating each of his first four birthdays in a different country, it was time to settle down. I owed it to him and to us.

The stress of having to look for a job had a stranglehold on me. I began my job hunt even before I had fully recovered from jet lag. Our meagre savings wouldn't last long. I was willing to take up anything: waiting tables at a restaurant, bagging groceries, even flipping burgers at McDonald's. A sales professional and ex–hotel manager, I would have cringed at the thought of doing this back home. I still did.

I had to remind myself, how much dignity would I have if my money ran out? Or worse, if I had to go back home and face the taunts of relatives who'd circle me like a flock of vultures? "I told you so" echoed in my mind in a myriad of voices.

"India was not good enough for you?" a crotchety aunt would ask.

"Came back with your tails between your legs ... serves you right," my cousin would say. "Can't say I didn't warn you."

"Welcome! Welcome back!" This from a distant uncle who'd most definitely have a condescending smirk on his face. "The lost travellers have returned."

Insomnia was a constant companion.

I eagerly grabbed all the free employment newspapers I could lay my hands on. I called various companies to get the names of their HR (human resources) managers before I sent out applications. People tripped over my name. Sometimes I corrected them, sometimes not. It didn't matter. What did matter was that I got the information I wanted, and most times I did.

One advertisement looked promising: a home-based business, no experience needed, everything provided. All a person needed was drive and motivation. I was ecstatic! I had oodles of both—I was a born saleswoman! I sent off my application.

The second advertisement was for a part-time recruiter at an IT (information technology) consulting firm. I had done recruiting back in the Middle East, but not in IT. I sent off my résumé anyway.

Both companies replied, and I landed two job interviews within days of arriving in Canada.

Too scared to travel on the subway alone, I asked my father to accompany me to the interview. I had peace of mind knowing there was someone to take me back "home." Even though I had lived in cities all my life, this place felt different. This was a fast-paced metro halfway across the world whose pulse and rhythm I would have to learn afresh. I wished I could fast-forward to a time when I too would jostle my way on to the subway, coffee in hand; read the paper as the stations whizzed past; alight at the right one; and not hesitate a moment as I headed toward the exit, my feet treading the route long before my mind realized where they were taking me.

On the day of the first interview, we arrived at a ramshackle building on Eglinton Avenue. We took a creaking elevator up to the second floor, where a man in cheap, ostentatious clothes ticked my name off on a clipboard (I was listed as Mr. Mahtab) and herded us into a room that was rapidly filling up. To my surprise, he even invited my father to attend. When the flood of job seekers had diminished to a trickle, the man shut the doors and the "presentation" began.

Within the first five minutes I wanted to escape. Escape immediately! The home-based business entailed selling perfumes of a very dubious quality, door to door. *And* I had to recruit strangers to help me sell; it was called pyramid marketing and apparently would make me rich. I was mortified. The perfumes made me sick, and around me, many a face had a greenish tinge. The presenter gassed us for over an hour. I fervently prayed I wouldn't throw up and embarrass myself. At the end of the presentation, I hurried past the sign-up sheet. McDonald's was preferable to this!

Outside, I gulped in a lungful of non-perfumed air. My heart spiralled down to my numb toes as I surveyed the cold, grey sky with not a hint of sunshine. What would the second interview be like?

The next day I headed downtown to interview with the IT firm. My father accompanied me once again and waited in the lobby while I went upstairs. Shortly afterwards I met the HR manager, an Indian! Within the first ten minutes we hit it off. She, too, was from Bombay, and it turned out that we had both attended the same school. She hired me on the spot and offered me a full-time sales job. With a light heart I raced back to the lobby to tell my father. Then we hurried home to tell the rest of the family and celebrated.

I started work on May 12, 1997. It was a moment of deep satisfaction. I had found a job within sixteen days of landing in Canada, in *my* profession. I was part of the workforce!

My job was to call clients in the United States and Canada and offer our services. Within the first few days there was a problem: my name. After many calls to the board line with clients asking for "Mata," "Martha," "Nadia," and even "some female, or maybe male whose name starts with the letter *m*," my supervisor told me to change my name to something easier, more Canadian.

I hated the idea.

I had managed to wrap my tongue around the most unusual names, had learned that Sean is pronounced "Shawn," and Siobhan, "Shivaughn." Why couldn't my clients at least try pronouncing mine? It wasn't so difficult, and I didn't care if they mispronounced it, as long as they tried!

You'd never have had this problem back home, a small voice nagged me. *Back home.... It was summer back home.* Crawford Market would be redolent with the fragrance of ripening Ratnagiri mangoes, golden orange and sweet as nectar. A bullock cart piled high with large, juicy watermelons would be winding its way through our narrow lane, tinkling bells heralding its approach. I thought longingly of Marine Drive, that wide swath of sun-baked sidewalk hugging the Arabian Sea, where I loved to walk during the monsoons. And the heat! I had given up all of that. Willingly.

And now I had to give up my name? It was like asking a tortoise to give up its shell. If I gave up my name, what would I be left with? Who would I be in this city of millions?

I suggested a solution: maybe I could speak slowly, spell out my name; it might work. My supervisor was adamant. I had to change it.

It was a request, but I knew I had no choice.

I agreed.

For the next few weeks, I tried to forget my real name, to forget who I was and become someone I was not. I had to remind myself constantly to answer to this name *I'd* chosen. I worked hard to create a brand-new identity in the corporate world of Canada.

"Hello. This is Maht—, Matty."

Those first few days, the greeting was always ragged, stilted, as if my lips were rebelling against what I'd made up my mind to do.

And so I became Matty, a name I tried not to whisper when I introduced myself. I tried hard to quash the tiny voice inside me that sang out "fraud" each time I said it. As it turns out, changing my name or myself wasn't such a bad thing after all, but I was not to realize this till ten years had passed.

The next hurdle came fairly quickly. I knew how to recruit staff, but IT was completely new to me.

My colleague and mentor threw me off the deep end into the alphabet soup of the IT world. I woke up at night in a cold sweat trying to remember what SOAP or J2EE meant. Every day we'd get job orders and a different set of acronyms that I had to memorize and match to a candidate who had worked with those technologies. It was a steep, steep learning curve. Often I felt that I was drowning in that soup!

Learning to respect the brutal cold of Canada didn't take as long. The day it seemed my scalp was two sizes too small for my head and a dentist's drill was piercing my eardrums, I learned that you *do not* go out with wet or even damp hair during winter, especially when it's windy.

In Bombay, sunshine and warmth stroll hand in hand, much like lovers along the Chowpatty beach. Not so in Canada. They don't even talk to each other here except occasionally in the summer. Wearing only a thin coat, I walked out of my building on a radiant spring morning and went from warm to shock in one second. Never again did I forget to check the weather before stepping out.

The occasional beggars at the street corner baffled me. They looked affluent, some even better dressed than the immigrants I had seen. They needed to go to India to see what poverty was all about. These guys hadn't a clue how lucky they were!

Summer flitted past before I realized it, and all too soon the dreaded winter was upon us. The chill of those short, dark days permeated our hearts. My husband and I talked about going back home. Life was just too hard here. Had we made a colossal mistake immigrating to Canada? Those days we had very few friends. There was no time or energy for anything but keeping our heads above water. Having family here gave us the strength to go on.

Gradually, I became aware of other unspoken forms of etiquette and acceptance. I felt puzzled and hurt when I would board a packed subway car or elevator and see people back away. On one occasion, I even got a rude sniff and a malevolent glare. I was shocked! A few weeks later I solved the mystery.

On my way to visit a friend, I boarded the elevator with an Indian couple. The smell of stale spices and garlic came off them in waves, poisoning the enclosed space. I could barely draw breath. How could they smell so pungent and not realize it? And then the thought struck me with the force of an avalanche, this is what I must smell like to others. Cooking with aromatic spices, without ventilation and Febreze, is an olfactory disaster!

I chalked up a huge laundry bill in the next few weeks as I dry cleaned or washed every item of clothing we owned and emptied the local Walmart of their entire supply of Febreze. To this day, I do not cook very aromatic dishes in winter when I have to keep the windows shut. If the urge to eat *dhunsak*, my favourite Parsi dish, overwhelms me, I throw open the windows and brave the chill while I cook. I religiously do the "nose test" when I wear my winter jacket. Febreze graces every closet in my home. I have my fellow countrymen to thank for this.

Another year crawled by. It was slow going because I simply could not keep up to the fast-paced IT industry. I tried to see myself as my clients did: a confident, determined woman, who answered to the name of Matty and promised to deliver on any skill set they asked for. And yet, I was not quite comfortable; I still felt like a fraud. And I missed Mahtab. A lot.

I remembered the time I had worked in the hotel industry in India, years ago. The endless shifts, the leering guests, and the constant need to apologize when it wasn't even my fault had worn me down till I couldn't stand it anymore. I had quit.

The same feeling overwhelmed me. Mahtab wanted to quit, once again.

I brushed up my résumé and started my job search in earnest. Surely there was something easier than this. And what might that be? the Matty voice inside me piped up. Isn't every new job tough at the beginning? I couldn't argue with that logic, but it didn't stop me from searching.

During a rough period when sales were at an all-time low, my supervisor yelled at us. "You call yourselves salespeople? I'm going to fire each and every one of you! YOU'RE ALL USELESS."

The only thing I heard was, "*You* are useless."

His words cut a lot deeper than the cold wind had, my first day in Canada. They lingered in my mind like a bad smell. I had *never* been fired from a job. Could I live with the indignity? Should I quit before it happened, just as I had done before? Was I doomed to be a quitter all my life? It was a time of deep soul-searching and much agony.

A memory surfaced from eons past: a visitor to our home had declared that he could read palms and predict one's character. A curious teenager, I had proffered my hand and immediately regretted it. His sweaty hands kneaded mine while he studied me with a piercing gaze. He told me that I had a very strong will and would succeed in whatever I put my mind to. I had great things in store for me, he said, but not without hard work. I had smiled politely as I extricated my hand, wondering if he was just a touch senile. Me and great things? Nah!

But what if he was right?

I decided that I would "allow" myself to quit only when I was at the very top of the sales team. Matty was not a quitter. I had come too far and lost too much to give up now.

I threw myself into the job with everything I had. Within a couple of years I became really good at sales, talking technical lingo with ease and, wonder of wonders, enjoying it. In the process I made a crucial discovery. I could do *anything* I put my mind to, and it had been as easy (or difficult) as wanting it badly enough.

Promotions came in rapid succession: assistant manager, manager, director, and finally vice-president. Now that I was at the top of the mountain, I could quit in style. The funny thing is, I didn't want to. I was having too much fun. Life would be smooth sailing from now on.

I was so wrong.

In 2003 I lost my father to cancer, swiftly and suddenly. It was a devastating moment. But it was also a time when I found out what I was really passionate about—writing.

I sought solace in books to cope with my loss. I read a lot, especially fantasy fiction. As each day went by, I would think of life back in Bombay when we had had fun as a family. I wanted to record it all, so I would never forget. My initial scribblings morphed into the idea of writing a children's book.

It took me a year and a half to write the book. Writing was hard, but the even harder part was trying to sell the manuscript. Rejections poured in, and once again I wanted to give up.

Mahtab would have. But Matty wouldn't let her. Not this time.

I joined a critique group and polished my manuscript again and again and yet again. Four years and twenty drafts later, *The Third Eye*, a fantasy adventure based in India, was published.

I decided to publish the book under my real name: Mahtab Narsimhan. After all, the protagonist had shades of the person I had once been. It felt great to be back, even if only in story form.

I had despised Matty once, for pushing me to do what I wasn't good at, for not letting me give up on a job that had made me miserable. I hadn't realized how valuable that lesson of never giving up had been. Matty made me succeed in the one thing that mattered to me above all else, my dream to be an author.

Mahtab and Matty—two very different personalities and, yet, codependent. They are both with me now and at peace with each other. The best part is, I can call upon one or the other as the occasion demands.

There is one more thing I need to learn. Once more.

"Hello, my name is Matt—, Mahtab."

The taste of my real name is delicious, a once-loved flavour I had almost forgotten. Bittersweet.

The Languages
I've Learned

DIMITRI NASRALLAH

I was eleven years old when, in August 1988, I arrived in Canada
for the first time. I was, just then, entering a dangerously
awkward period of my life, an in-betweener collection of years
in which my childhood, once so seemingly simple and carefree,
was transforming into a series of empty, self-conscious acts.
He-Man, the solar system, good grades, dinosaurs, parental
advice, lions, friendship—nothing was as reassuring as it had
once been, and I grew estranged from everyone, myself
included. In the midst of these fundamental complications in
my personality, we moved to the city of Montreal, which my
parents had billed as the solution to our homelessness. When
we got there, we huddled in cramped apartments for a year,
living as mice do between walls.

For the first month, we lived in a small, furnished one-
bedroom on the first floor of a high-rise apartment on Milton
Street, in the heart of the McGill ghetto. It was an apartment
that would have otherwise been suited to a single twenty-
something slumming through an education paid for by parents'
savings. My sister and I shared the bedroom, while my mother

and father slept on a fold-out sofa bed in what was, during the daytime, our living room. In that month, my parents collected all the necessary items we would need to start a life, and my sister—still a tomboy who copied my every move—and I tried to imagine what our lives would be like at school that September. Our first major purchases were two single beds, a desk, a sofa bed, and a TV: a solid foundation my parents had learned to depend on in past moves.

I suppose it was all a bit methodical, but we had moved several times by then, and so there was an element to the settling that we had invariably done before. Canada was the third country we had lived in that year alone. Before Canada, we had been living in Dubai for the summer, over ten thousand kilometres away, waiting for my father to complete a contract for an advertising company. He had been living in Dubai on his own for a year already by the time we joined him from Athens, where he'd lost his job. We had always recognized Greece as our temporary home and had never planned for the country to sustain us as long as it did. Dubai became an even more temporary one, all because we were still waiting out a civil war in Lebanon, which by then was into its thirteenth year. It was older than I was, and I had been born into it. My parents hadn't ever intended to settle down in Athens, but by the time we were forced to move again, we had lived there seven years, and Greece was my home.

We were the perpetual visitors of other countries. That was the design of our lives. For as long as I can remember, and even before that, it had always been this way. There were times in my early life, before I had a memory at all, spent in Kuwait and in Athens, and there were times before I was born that my parents had spent in Saudi Arabia, waiting out bad episodes of infighting. But, for me, these events were background, moulded by my toddler's curiosity and penetrating my oblivious world in sudden bursts of anger or sadness, or through the stray stories of other travellers. Relatives would die, apartments would be lost to squatters or simply destroyed, cars would explode, and in the meantime we would wait. By the time we arrived in Montreal, we had lived in more than a few furnished apartments and hotels. What was different this time was that my parents had effectively given up on waiting any longer.

It is there, on the very edges of my memory: my parents' fourth-floor apartment in Ras, Beirut, the home where I was born. I had an aunt and an uncle who lived on the second floor, and they had a barbershop in their apartment where I would get my hair cut and play with my cousins. That apartment had, in a sense, always been there, waiting to become my real home too. I remember many things about those early years, memories dimly lit and crudely coloured by the imagination of being under the age of five, when much of what I needed to know could still be turned into a game.

I remember, for example, the summer before we left Beirut, in 1982. We had been staying at a hotel in the hills that had been bombed several times, once leaving a gaping hole in the tennis courts. I remember there was one night when bombs started to fall during a holiday, and we had been sitting on our balcony, shooting fireworks into the night air. Everyone at the hotel was out on this clear night and bringing the sky to life with red and yellow displays of decorative explosions. All of a sudden, the balcony shook violently, and we learned that one of the explosions was real, and then another. They had become expected punctuation to our ordinary life, and so when we were bombed, we always had an escape ready, if only for a night at a time. I remember that even I had a plan, hatched one quiet afternoon on a playground behind the hotel while swinging in the shade of old willow trees, and that night I put it to use for the first time: I ran into the bathroom to hide. My father yanked the door open and grabbed me by the collar and, with my baby sister tucked under his arm like a drooling football, ran down to the cellars, dragging me behind him all the way.

The day we left Lebanon we took a taxi down from the mountains, to the Beirut harbour. We drove through a part of the city that we had lived in only months previous, and I barely recognized what was left of our old street. The buildings were all shelled, the stores beneath them gutted or shuttered, and all that was left in the empty, silent streets was the skeletons of cars covered in the thick dust of blasted cement. At the ferry waiting to take us away, soldiers ran the lines—I didn't know whose soldiers they were, and it wouldn't have made a difference to me. Sleeping on deck chairs under a starlit sky, our suitcases burrowing between our legs, we stole away from the city that was home. The next day we landed in Cyprus, and two days later we flew to Athens and began our second lives.

I was, back in 1982, still too young to have friends of my own. I had yet to spend enough time at schools in Beirut to know anyone from there, and in any case the schools were often cancelled. The world I knew contained mainly my parents and my sister. Beyond them, I knew only aunts, uncles, cousins, and grandparents, who soon became shadows in my life abroad.

Athens, at that age and in late August, essentially meant for me going to school and exploring the world independently for the first time, if only for a few hours at a time. Attending kindergarten was made doubly difficult by certain factors that were well outside my control. For one, I did not speak English, the language of the American international school I began attending in September of that year.

Not only did I not speak a word of English, but just before the first day of school, as my sister and I were chasing a tennis ball across our new bedroom in downtown Athens, I tripped over her snatching hands and dug my forehead into the sharp end of an old radiator. We hadn't even been in the country for more than two weeks, and my father didn't know where to find a hospital. He quickly wrapped my bleeding head in a towel and, not knowing a word of Greek himself, carried me down four flights of stairs, hailed a taxi, and trusted in the goodwill of strangers to get him and a bloody boy to the nearest emergency room. It worked, but I missed the first day of kindergarten, and when I finally did go on the second day, my head was wrapped tightly in white gauze, with a vague crimson stain seeping through where a doctor had sewn together the two flaps of my forehead.

To the strangers I encountered on that second day of school, many from nationalities and ethnicities I'd never before known, I must have looked like a newly branded calf: behind the lines, half-wobbling, disoriented, and marked plainly for all to see, on my forehead no less, as different. I had no way to communicate with even my teacher, who had to resort to hand signals and the charity of the other Arab five-year-olds in our class, who translated on her behalf. That day couldn't end fast enough. But steadily, over the next year, I did manage to learn English, and the language came to me easily, as languages often will to young children. By the end of my seven years, I had even grown quite skilled at it.

No one who passed through that international school ever stayed for longer than three or four years. Students came from as far and wide as the United States and Japan, or just happened to be Greek and rich. They were contractors' kids, army-base kids, embassy kids, Mafia kids, or simply waiting-room kids like me, whose parents were more interested in getting away from one place than actually settling down somewhere else.

In this waiting room of a country, between the ages of five and twelve, English became my barometer, and eventually I began to think and dream in the language of my educators. Neither of my parents spoke English at home, though my mother was studying it privately, and so I was tacitly encouraged to practise it on my own by reading the many English books my mother bought for me. I fell in love with reading that way, first with picture books and then with books that had only words. Eventually, English also became the language I shared with my sister.

Arabic became my parents' language, a language for home and Sunday school and the weekly Arabic classes given at the international school. Later, Greek became the language of the streets below our apartment building, where we often played hide-and-seek with the neighbourhood children, and where we spent long, hot summer afternoons building forts in the shade of abandoned construction sites and crushing cans for games of soccer in the warm evening air. I got good enough at Greek to read comic books.

Each of those languages had its place, and somehow it made me happier to have these barriers of privacy in my life. I got older and the war faded away, out of my day-to-day existence. In every grade, I would meet others who stumbled in just as I had, without a word of English and terribly unprepared. I would watch them grapple with hand signals toward their first words, and I would wonder how I'd ever managed.

And then, suddenly, it was my turn once again. Canada. When I first learned that my family would move, I was elated. At long last, the wait was coming to an end! The news meant that I would finally hand over my reign of longest-running student at the international school to one of the two or three other kids in my grade who'd been there since that kindergarten class. I had literally hundreds of questions about Canada, and quickly I turned the place into the land of everything I'd ever wanted but never had, all before setting foot on the tarmac at Mirabel airport. But once the immigration applications were in order and we finally arrived in Montreal and I began to attend a new school, I realized that my new life was going to be drastically different than I could've ever imagined. Canada was, for the first few years, a grave disappointment.

To begin with, there was the conspicuous matter of being held back one year, on account of the different age criteria Quebecois schools used for dividing grades. Then there was the fact that I would be forced to continue my education in French, even though I spoke no French and there were perfectly good English-language schools nearby, all because my parents hadn't studied in English. This became, in my mind, the first of my parents' many faults. At eleven years old, I knew very little of Quebec's cultural history or the reasoning behind Bill 101, and so I was convinced that the French language had been thrust at me in ambush by my parents, who had lied to further their own interests.

As my twelfth birthday came and went, I grew more and more suspicious of the world. Apparently, what I'd assumed was my birthday wasn't actually my birthday after all. Among the many undesirable truths I'd learned about my family during the move to our third life was the little secret that my official birthday—the one on my documents—had me listed as being six months younger than I actually was. I had trouble wrapping my head around how this could've happened to me without my ever knowing, and why my parents had never told me of this second, more important, birthday all this time. They were evasive in telling me why this was, and in my mind it fell into the same conspiracy of my parents' arranging to get me into a French school. They said it hadn't ever made any difference before, but in Canada everything my parents had never told me began to make all the difference in the world. Nothing was meant to stay the same, and everything—birthdays and languages included— would sooner or later come up for change.

I changed schools three times that first year, in what would become one of the worst years of my life. The first school I attended for only three days, and nothing there made sense to me. To highlight my inability to fit in, I was assigned to a special classroom for new immigrants. This particular school had only two such classrooms, and so every child in the building between grades three and six who was new to the country was dumped into the same class. This meant that not only would I not be in the seventh grade, as I believed I was entitled to be, but I had to learn my fourth language alongside doodling seven- and eight- year-olds, among them my little sister.

At an age when I was just beginning to crave privacy for the first time, there was suddenly nowhere to hide. Even in the bathroom, someone was bound to knock on the door after ten minutes. How could the end of our waiting years, which had been so leisurely, turn out to be so unfair? In Canada, it seemed to me, we were poorer, we were less happy, and, because of the size of our apartment, we were always crawling over one another's belongings and were never more than five feet apart.

The school we moved to on the fourth day at least put my sister and me in separate classes, and from that point on I threw myself into the apparently impossible task of trying to fit into a province where the language laws stated that all the languages I knew meant nothing to the teachers in those immigrant classes or to the students in the other rooms. I had to work harder than ever to muster up enough French to get out of that special class and into my third school that year. Like our small apartment, there was only so much room in my life for languages; therefore, to make room for what I had to learn, I began to let go of the Arabic and Greek I knew, if only because in Canada there was no use for that kind of knowledge. Arabic slowly faded away as the language of our home, as my parents threw themselves into their new lives by letting go of everything that had come before.

By January, I had learned enough French to move to my third school, where I would attend my first normal classes in Canada. It was there that I began noticing girls for the first time. As this new distraction entered my life, my preoccupations shifted to a skinny Vietnamese girl whose name was Dong Thui. Soon after that, I began to leave my own head more regularly, and even my obsession with privacy began to develop little methods of dealing with our tiny apartment. Every morning when I woke up, I would go over to the only possession I owned as my very own, my prized typewriter. And, as I waited my turn for the bathroom, I would type with no sheet of paper, onto the black wheel, "I LOVE YOU DONG THUI," and I would leave that there, invisible, for no one to see, and go brush my teeth for school. It was my first deliberate act of independence: writing for no other reason than the words would never be read. I did that every morning, and it became part of my education.

The language problem proved more resistant than we'd expected. So, we picked up our third lives and moved again to the other Canada, to Toronto and to English Canada, two years after we arrived in Montreal. By then we had an even stronger

sense of what to expect, for we knew the method and the disap-
pointments that come with learning ever-newer ways of leading
ordinary lives. And so we started over on our fourth lives.
Coming to Canada, I learned that when lives change, they do not
always escape cleanly from their pasts, that sometimes soft
indentures in the shape of letters are left behind on the black
wheel of their memories, and that at other times lives are
scarred by unpoetic and sudden gashes, and these in turn build
a personality.

Many years have passed. I've since moved back to Montreal, on
my own this time, and Canada does feel something like a home,
even though it is a very different home depending on where you
happen to be in the country.

As I got older and entered my teens, I grew alienated from my
parents for some years. I began to think of them as being from
another world, and I decided that I was not like them. My
parents belonged to an older generation and an antiquated way
of thinking, and as a result they did things differently than I
would have done them. It was not merely age; they weren't
anything like the parents of my friends either. They came from
a history that shadowed us, but that no longer existed outside
their minds. I knew that hidden world, too. But unlike them, I
was young enough to have room for two worlds in my life: the
reclusive past that survived in the suburban townhouse my
parents bought four years after arriving in Canada, and the
wide-open future outside its front door. I saw possibilities out
there. My life out there, increasingly opportunistic, became a
delicately tended secret. I became one person for my parents
and quite another to everyone else. I longed to escape their
suburban townhouse, and yet something deep inside always

compelled me to shield our home from the outside world, *my* outside world. I couldn't be the one to corrupt their hard work for them.

And then, thirteen or fourteen years later, I realized that the very person I'd been trying to become all those years was precisely the one I'd left behind, back in that tiny fourth-floor apartment of my most distant memories. By then, I had grown more like my parents than I would have ever thought possible. I was thinking of having my own children, and suddenly it was me who was from a different place. I had come full circle to the question of how much of my roots I would reveal to my own children, how I would instill roots in the lives of others. No one ever tells you that fitting in never ends. It happens everywhere I go, or every time I try something new. It is a lifelong struggle. It will happen to you, too.

Crossing
Yonge Street

MARINA NEMAT

When I was about fifteen years old, my brother, Alik, who had immigrated to Canada, wrote to me about Yonge Street. Back then I lived in Tehran, Iran, where I was born. Alik told me that Yonge Street was about 1900 kilometres long and was the longest street in the world. This was unimaginable for me. I was always an avid reader, and as I tried to picture it in my mind, I saw the yellow brick road leading to the Emerald City in *The Wizard of Oz*. Yonge Street had to be full of mystery and adventure.

Alik left for Canada shortly after the success of the Islamic Revolution in Iran in 1979. He was fourteen years older than I, had a university degree, and wanted a better life. When he decided to leave Iran, he and his wife chose Canada because they believed it was a good and free country.

When I was sixteen, I was arrested by the Revolutionary Guard for speaking up against the government of Iran. I spent two years, two months, and twelve days as a political prisoner in Tehran's notorious Evin prison. Before prison, I had plans to become a medical doctor, but after Evin, this became impossible. It was very difficult to enter a university with a political record. Even if I were somehow accepted, the authorities would watch my every move and continue their efforts to turn me into an obedient citizen, and I couldn't tolerate that after all the brainwashing I had already been subjected to. I couldn't keep my mouth shut, and I knew I would always be in danger of being arrested again if I went back to school.

I needed out.

After my release, however, the government of Iran refused to give me a passport, and I had to wait six years for permission to leave the country. One might argue that, like many others, I could have paid a human smuggler to take me across the border into Turkey or Pakistan, but there were two main reasons why this was not the right solution for me. The first was that my parents couldn't afford the fee. And the second was that I had already been tortured, raped, and shot at. People died trying to cross the Iranian border illegally. Many were arrested by either Iranian or Pakistani or Turkish authorities. I had had enough of that. I wanted to get on an airplane like a normal human being. I wanted to buckle up like it was nothing and munch on salted almonds as I left my life and my country behind.

The Islamic Revolution succeeded when I was thirteen, and it turned our world upside down. I was from a Christian family. I grew up during the time of the shah (the king of Iran who had tried to Westernize the country), and I loved to watch *Little House on the Prairie*, read Jane Austen, and listen to the Bee Gees. My family owned a cottage by the Caspian Sea, where I spent the last summer before the revolution flirting with boys and sunbathing on the beach in a bikini.

When we returned to Tehran from the cottage that summer, I watched the Islamic Revolution unfold from my window. It was a slow drizzle at first but soon turned into a flash flood, engulfing the streets, washing away the normalcy of our lives. Our street, which had always been congested with cars and filled with pedestrians, who strolled or rushed along or haggled with vendors, became empty and silent. Even the beggars were gone. Military trucks shadowed every corner. Once every few days, hundreds of angry demonstrators filled the street, bearded men leading the way and women wearing chadors following them; with their fists raised in the air, they screamed, "Down with the shah!" and "Independence, freedom, Islamic republic!" For the first time in my life, I heard shots fired; the military had opened fire on demonstrating crowds.

Even though the revolution was gathering momentum and we were all worried, my parents believed that a bunch of mullahs and unarmed civilians would never defeat the shah's military. But they were wrong. The shah went into exile. Ayatollah Khomeini, who had become the leader of the revolution and had been in exile for years, returned to Iran. The Islamic republic was born, and with it, our world and all the rules that had held it together collapsed. Dancing was declared satanic. My father, who had been a ballroom-dancing instructor, was forced to work as an office clerk at a stainless-steel factory. He hated his new job, but he was hopeful that the new Islamic government would not last long. Soon, makeup, pretty clothes, and Western books became illegal. And, before I knew it, fanatic young women from the Revolutionary Guard, most of whom didn't even have a high school diploma, had replaced the wonderful teachers of my high school. These unqualified new teachers filled most of the class time with political rhetoric. When I protested, I was told that I could leave the classroom if I didn't like the new order of things. I did, and, by doing so, I unintentionally began a school-wide strike that went on for three days.

During the next few months, I started a school newspaper and wrote articles against the government. Our new principal, who was only nineteen years old and a member of the Revolutionary Guard, came to see me as one of her worst enemies. Most of my friends were now supporters of Marxist or Marxist-Islamist political groups, and I tried very hard to fit in with them, but, even though I hated the new government, I was a devout Christian who attended mass every day. So, I soon found myself isolated and depressed. My parents were aware of most of my activities, but they never tried to stop me; after all, by our old normal standards, I wasn't doing anything wrong. All I wanted was to study math, science, and literature instead of government propaganda and the Koran. Finally, the principal gave my name to the Courts of Islamic Justice, and I was arrested on January 15, 1982.

While in prison, I was forced to convert to Islam, but, shortly after my release, I returned to my church. According to the laws that govern Iran, once you convert to Islam, you are not allowed to return to your old religion. Because I had gone back to my church, I was automatically condemned to death. I lived with a death sentence hanging over my head.

About a year after my release, I married my boyfriend, Andre, who was the organist at my church. He had waited for me and had never lost hope that I would survive prison. Every single moment in Iran, I expected the Revolutionary Guard to show up at my door and take me back to Evin. I was terrified, but I strongly believed that I had every right to be who I was. My faith was stronger than my fear.

About three years after our marriage, Andre and I had a son, whom we named Michael. We finally managed to leave Iran when he was just under two years old.

Getting through the airport security in Tehran was nerve-racking. We could have been denied exit or even been arrested. But they let us through. Security guards searched every piece of luggage by hand. Passengers were not allowed to take large sums of money, antiques, or anything that seemed expensive. My wedding photos were in an album that was a gift from a friend. It was handmade of Italian leather and was one of the most beautiful things I owned. I wanted to take it with me, but I was told that I wouldn't be allowed, so I dumped my wedding photos in a plastic bag and left the album behind. My grandmother, who had passed away when I was seven, had an antique silver jewellery box, which I adored. I loved my grandmother, and the box reminded me of her, but I couldn't take it with me either.

First, we flew to Madrid, where we went to a Catholic refugee agency. They told us that it could take us about three years to make it to Canada, which was where we desperately wanted to go. Three years sounded like an eternity. When the people at the agency saw our disappointment, they gave us a letter of recommendation and suggested that we go directly to the Canadian embassy to present our case. Andre was an electrical engineer and had published papers in international magazines, we had good credentials, and we were both fluent in English.

At the Canadian embassy, once we mentioned that Andre's parents were Hungarians who had migrated to Iran for work and that we had family in Hungary, the secretary suggested that we go to Budapest and, from there, apply to come to Canada as immigrants. She told us that we were qualified and that the process from Budapest would be much quicker than from Madrid. We took her advice, and this was probably the wisest decision of our lives.

Ten months later, we were on our way to Canada. As our plane glided west over the Atlantic Ocean, I wondered what our new country was truly like. Alik had sent me photos of his house in the Toronto suburbs. His home was big—very big compared to the small apartments I had lived in most of my life—and looked so beautiful that it seemed fictional, but Alik told me that, according to Canadian standards, it was an average house. He had also sent me photos of Niagara Falls, the CN Tower, and the University of Toronto, but he might as well have sent me pictures of Narnia or some other imaginary land. All of Alik's photos seemed alien. Even Canada's colours were different from those of my life: the blues were deeper, the browns stronger, the reds more vibrant, the yellows sharper, the greens more alive, and the pinks and purples dreamier. Canada was another planet to me. A cold land where it snowed and snowed in winter and where summer was a little treasure tucked away at the shores of a blue lake surrounded by the emerald green of pine-covered hills. But how friendly was this magical land? Would we be able to find our way in its strange vastness?

Michael was about two and a half, and, thankfully, he slept for most of the flight. When he woke, we were close to Toronto. I told him to look out the window at the beautiful clouds.

"Is that Canada?" he asked, pointing at an enormous cumulonimbus cloud. I had told him so much about our new country that he was quite excited about it. I had promised him that we would make big snowmen in winter and swim in lakes in summer.

"No, honey, that's a cloud. Canada is down there ... below the clouds.... We can't see it yet."

"Snowman!" he cried, pointing at another cloud.

Even God makes snowmen here, I thought.

That day, the day I arrived in Canada, I wore my nicest dress. My mother had made it. It was burgundy and very stylish. I had even bought new shoes to go with it. They were black and had three-inch heels. I wanted to blend in with the crowd, to look Canadian. I believed that the people who lived in a wealthy country like Canada had to be very fashionable. As we made our way through Pearson airport, I was surprised to see that most women were wearing blue jeans or khaki pants. But it didn't matter. One should be well dressed when beginning a new life.

I wanted to mark the occasion properly. I had waited for this day for seven years.

I can't remember much about Pearson. My memory is a jumble of images: rushing along hallways with Michael in my arms, standing in lines, and answering an immigration officer's questions. Once we made it to the public concourse, I wanted to scream Alik's name out loud, but I contained myself. Although I had not seen him in twelve years, I immediately spotted him. His hair had greyed and thinned a little, but he was six foot seven, and his head bobbed over the enthusiastic chaos of the waiting crowd. We hugged and couldn't let go.

I sat in the back seat of Alik's car and stared at the scenery as we drove to his house. We were to stay at his place until we could find an apartment. The sky was indigo blue, as unrealistic as a child's painting. And the horizon seemed so far away, farther than I had ever seen it. It was August, and the fields were fluorescent green, the cornfields seeming to stretch all the way to the North Pole. Buildings were scarce, and the air was saturated with the scent of grass, water, and soil.

"Where's Toronto?" I asked Alik.

"Toronto!" Michael exclaimed, pointing at horses in a farmer's field.

"My house is in the suburbs," Alik said, as if this explained everything. We had suburbs in Tehran, but we had almost no open spaces between them. What I saw was farmland and wilderness.

The car moved along the highway, and, after a few minutes, a town with rows of almost identical brick houses came into view. We had arrived. I was worried but hopeful. How could I possibly not find my way to a good life in a land of so many intense colours? As we walked into Alik's house, I felt like an astronaut on her first Martian expedition.

The first time I took Michael to a park in Canada, it was drizzling. But we went anyway. In Hungary, people had sometimes called me "gypsy" and sworn at me on the bus or at the park. I didn't take it personally. I had nothing against gypsies, but I was not one. I had dark eyes and long dark hair, and I guessed that Hungarians had never seen an Iranian before. They had lived in a closed society for many years—we had arrived there right after the fall of Communism—and I couldn't blame them for it. I hoped that things were different in Canada and that I wouldn't be judged because of the colour of my hair or my skin.

I put Michael in a swing and pushed him as hard as I could. He laughed in delight. "Higher! Higher!" No one else was there, but after a few minutes, a man with a girl about Michael's age joined us. I guessed the man was the girl's grandfather. Michael got off the swing and went to the slide, and the man put the little girl in a swing. I watched them. The man smiled at me. I smiled an uncertain smile. He wore black casual pants and a beige jacket. Unlike me, he seemed very much at ease. He and the child blended in and were a part of Planet Canada, clearly not at all aware of its strangeness. Their every step told me that they knew what they were doing, while my every move was full of doubt and insecurity. How many times had they come to this park before? They had probably both been born in this country. This place belonged to them, and the truth was that I was an outsider—but, at least, I was sure that Michael would soon feel as though he had always lived here.

The rain had become heavier. The sky was the colour of a storm, an impatient shade of grey.

"Do you need a ride?" the man asked me.

I shook my head and mumbled a thank-you.

"Cookies! I want cookies!" Michael said. He had had his very first chocolate-chip cookie the day before, and we had no more left. I knew that there was a convenience store around the corner, but I had not bought anything in Canada yet, as we were still staying at my brother's house.

"Cookies! Please, please!" Michael begged, and I scooped him up in my arms and ran toward the store as the rain drew puddles on the sidewalk. "Rain, rain, go away, come again another day," I sang. I was teaching Michael English, and he loved nursery rhymes.

They had so many different types of cookies at the store that it took me a few minutes to find the right kind. I felt dizzy. The abundance astonished me. I prayed that Michael wouldn't want to try them all. Wide-eyed, he stared at the colourful, overflowing shelves. My eyes filled with tears, as I put the package in front of the cashier, a young blonde woman. I couldn't believe that I had become emotional buying cookies. I gave her a twenty-dollar bill. She had no idea how treacherous my life had been and how long I had waited to get here.

"What a cute little boy," she said, as she handed me my change. "Nice shoes! Where did you get them?"

Michael was in my arms, wearing a pair of multicoloured suede shoes I had bought in Hungary.

"In Europe," I said.

"I thought so. They don't make them so nice here. Where in Europe?"

"Hungary. We've just immigrated here."

"Do you like it so far?"

"Yes. Very much. People are nice."

I had gone to the park, now I was at the store, and no one had sworn at me. I had not been beaten up or arrested or both for not wearing the hijab or for any other reason. And we had bought cookies! What more could one ask for? Michael and I skipped all the way home, singing nursery rhymes. I knew that our life in Canada would not be a fairy tale. Fairy tales entail a certain kind of innocence that I had lost at sixteen, and since then, I had not believed in "happily ever after." But here, we could hope and work hard for a better life.

Andre found a job in his own field a few days after our arrival; this was close to a miracle because Canada was in recession at the time. We rented an apartment, paid our "first and last," and had two hundred dollars left in our bank account. Alik had bought us a loveseat and a chair, and we had bought a cheap dining table, six chairs, a bed for Michael, and a queen-size mattress, which we put on the floor in our bedroom. Andre's boss gave us an old TV that he was not using any longer, and we bent a metal clothes hanger and used it as an antenna. It gave us six channels, which was much better than the two channels we had had in Tehran. We were grateful for all we had.

As it turned out, the first apartment we rented in Canada happened to be on Yonge Street. I will never forget the very first time I stood at the pedestrian crossing at the intersection of Yonge Street and Baif Boulevard. It was late September or early October, and the sun still had a little bit of warmth. Michael was clinging to my hand, waiting, as impatiently as I, for the helpful little white man to appear and signal that it was safe to cross the street to go to the grocery store. Even though my house had not fallen on a wicked witch and a good witch had not given me ruby slippers, I felt like Dorothy at the beginning of her journey. The difference was that I knew that the wizard, no matter how powerful he was, could not take me back home. My home didn't want me any longer. But I had a journey ahead of me. I had to learn how to belong in Emerald City, and I had to find out why I had been chosen to survive and come this far.

Tales from
the Twilight Zone

RICHARD POPLAK

I never know where to sit. So I choose the middle. With my
shoulder to the wall. It's a technique I learned from an episode
of *Miami Vice*, in which hardened cop Sonny Crockett tells
partner Ricardo Tubbs that he never sits with his back to the
crowd. This way, he can keep an eye out for danger, whip out his
gun, shoot first. "No surprises," says Crockett. This is a man
who drives a Ferrari Daytona, lives on a yacht, and keeps an
alligator as a pet. I will not argue with his reasoning. So I choose
the middle. With my shoulder to the wall.

And I stare at the black girl.

Most of the kids remove their jackets, drop their knapsacks,
pull out a notebook. The black girl does the same. I keep my
jacket on, pull it tight around me. The wall is sharp with cold;
cold travels into the classroom on thin beams of sunlight. The
air quickly turns stuffy, but the wall beside me refuses to warm
up. Crockett never mentioned this phenomenon to Tubbs,
possibly because Miami, like my old hometown, does not share
weather with Toronto. Back in Johannesburg, our classrooms
would consume the winter sun in large gulps through windows

that overlooked drought-dry playing fields. We were not permitted to keep our blazers on in class, no matter how cold it became. So we would shiver through early-morning classes, waiting for the day to warm up. It always warmed up.

No surprises.

I watch the black girl. She is long and lean limbed, and she laughs easily, throwing her head back and closing her eyes. The teacher looks at her sternly; she is causing a disturbance. The black girl drops her voice and finishes her sentence in a stage whisper. Her hair is arranged in tight braids that cascade over the plastic of her desk and chair. Now she opens her notebook, all business.

I do not reach into my knapsack for a notebook. What we will learn here today means nothing to me. In the old country, it was hip to wear our knapsacks low, so that they swung against our butts as we walked. It is not cool to do so here. At home, it was forbidden to defile our knapsacks with the names of our favourite bands. Here, this is normal. The black girl's knapsack says SONIC YOUTH. I have never heard of Sonic Youth.

The teacher writes a squiggle of nonsense on the board, his chalk sending puffs of dust into the thick air. He talks, his moustache flapping up and down. I think of an episode of *The Twilight Zone* in which a man wakes up one morning to learn that everyone he knows speaks a language that is incomprehensible to him. He cannot read street signs, nor can he understand his colleagues, his wife, his young daughter. He is terrified. At the end of the episode, he sits at his daughter's bedside, reading her a story. Tears well up in his eyes as he mumbles the words in her nursery book. Slowly, he is learning. I guess that this episode was trying to say something positive about the human spirit.

I go back to staring at the black girl. She has raised her hand and is waving it vigorously in answer to a question I did not hear. I stand up abruptly, knocking my table forward. And I make for the door, thinking, *What does this say about the human spirit?*

The librarian tells me I cannot eat in the library. She tells me this when I am halfway through a sandwich, three-quarters of the way through lunch period, almost all the way through my sanity. She points to a sign that reads NO EATING IN THE LIBRARY.

This is bad news, because I don't want to join the crowds in the cafeteria. It's not like it is in the movies: new boy mocked by the cool kids, tray knocked over, milk spilled, embarrassment. No one yells *Nerrrrrrrrrrrd!* No one yells anything. And I think I know why this may be.

It's exactly like something my favourite comic-book character, Rorschach, says to his fellow inmates after he's been framed for murder and thrown in prison in chapter six of *Watchmen*. After unleashing unholy violence on some poor sap in the lunchroom lineup, he offers the following menacing utterance: *None of you understand. I'm not locked up in here with you. You're locked up in here with ME!*

I have been at this school for five days. Claude Watson School of the Arts, Toronto, Canada. It feels more like five years. It has been a lesson in the meaninglessness of time. I'm not capable of unholy violence, but my fellow inmates (a) don't know this and (b) can sense that I am a different from your average social outcast.

It starts, I am almost sure, with my clothing. I remember the day we bought it. My father drove us along scorching tarmac to a mall on the outskirts of Johannesburg, in a suburb called

Randfontein. Deep inside the mall, toward the service entrance away from the big-name stores, stood a ski shop. This was, arguably, the most useless store in the city. It had snowed in Johannesburg only once in fifteen years, a paltry inch of fluff that buried the dust of the city and transformed all life into a euphoric carnival for the duration of one perfectly white afternoon.

Of cold, I knew only the brittle Johannesburg winter mornings that sent me from bed to the anthracite heater in order to hastily don my grey socks, grey school slacks, white button-up shirt, green tie, green blazer with school crest, polished black shoes. The ski store represented another reality. It suggested the mythical land of Canada, where all my friends would be as hip and interesting as the cast of *Fame*, wear leotards as a matter of course, spontaneously break into synchronized dance numbers, and smoke unfiltered French cigarettes while reciting the lyrics of "Hotel California."

"This one," I said to the salesperson, picking out a turquoise-on-blue jacket that, in retrospect, looked like something Stalin would wear if he went skiing. My boots too had a dictator-in-the-snow vibe about them. Along with my acid-washed jeans, sweaters that looked like Smartie upchuck, and *Top Gun* haircut, I was ready for action. That is, assuming we were moving to Yugoslavia.

I'm dressed this way when I skulk from the library into the hallway, pushing the rest of my sandwich into my mouth, gazing in wonder at the lunch-hour mayhem. Kids huddle together, yelling brightly. There is a frenzied litter of cans and wrappers around them; their world is as colourful as that of a Saturday morning cartoon.

And these kids come in different colours. They intermingle and weave in and out of one another's lives. They cross paths, shake hands, hug. White hands, yellow hands, black hands. I come from the land of separation. I am a child of apartheid, from a country where no white kid and no black kid have ever shared the hallway of a school together. And down this particular hallway walks the black girl—the one from math class. She looks the other way as I pass her by.

I think she knows. She knows that she is locked up in here with me.

I am supposed to be an artist. This is what people tell me. And this is why I stand in the workshop with a naked mannequin before me. Claude Watson School for the Arts is a school for artistic people.

Thing is, I'm not so sure about the art caper. Granted, since I was a young boy, I could draw well. My nursery school teachers marvelled at my ability to render Superman's cape, Spider-Man's intricate webbing, Wonder Woman's lustrous hair. Later, I studied under the harsh eye of Mrs. Macilrath. (Note the "wrath" buried in her name.) Her mantra was *Look, look again, draw what you see.* She placed the stuffed inhabitants of her strange dead menagerie before us, and I would look, look again, and draw what I saw. I saw angora rabbits, meerkats, creatures I cannot name and have no wish to. Dutifully, I drew what I saw.

In her handbag, Mrs. Macilrath kept a great, burnished silver .44 Ruger Special handgun with a laser sighting and a spare clip for emergencies. This was a big gun, something that Sonny Crockett would use in *Miami Vice* to blow away bad guys. Mrs. Macilrath kept it because you just never knew. You never knew when *they* were coming for you.

Who *they* were never needed to be said.

At Claude Watson, the art teacher does not carry a semi-automatic weapon. He does not insist that we draw what we see.

He wears tight black slacks and a black turtleneck—finally, someone who looks like a cast member of *Fame*. Our task is to transform our mannequins into creatures of our wildest imaginations. One student has inserted a small black-and-white television into the belly of her mannequin. It plays a loop of a fashion model walking up and down a runway. "It's a comment on the interplay of eating and the fashion industry," says the girl.

I have no idea what this means.

I stare down at my mannequin, who stares blankly back at me. Every time I pick her up, her frozen arms lock around by neck, my head conks with her unforgiving noggin. It's an awkward dance, and the art teacher looks at me sympathetically. "Done much sculpture work?" he asks. I look across the art class at all the students working away on their mannequins. The black girl makes sure to avoid my eye, something she is becoming very good at. Over the smooth, globular breasts of her mannequin—who is wearing a dog collar and leash—she has scrawled the words FREE MANDELA.

I resist the urge to run from the class. I yank at my mannequin's right arm, and it comes free with a satisfying crack.

"That's it!" says the teacher encouragingly. "Get right in there."

I stare at the arm. I grab a roll of black electrical tape. It squeals like an animal in pain as I unspool it, strapping the arm to the mannequin's head. "Nice!" says the teacher. "I like what that says."

What, I wonder, does a mannequin with an arm taped to its head "say"? Am I tapping deep into my subconscious, "disarming" my old self and being created anew in this brand-new, icy country?

The art teacher seems to me like every movie shrink I've ever watched onscreen. How can something that doesn't talk "say" anything? Does he speak to rocks? Birds? Motor vehicles? His world is one of conversation with inanimate objects, single-cell organisms, invertebrates, hacked-apart mannequins. All that unstoppable, unending nattering would send me to the loony bin. What the art teacher needs, I keep thinking, is some silence.

When I start tearing a leg off, he slowly backs away. I don't think he likes what I'm saying.

Her name is Cynthia.

I have never known the name of a black girl my age. I hadn't really considered the possibility that she *had* a name before I heard one of her friends call out to her after math class.

Cynthia.

What does Cynthia do after school? What are her parents like? Other than Sonic Youth—whoever they may be—what are her interests? The girl is a cipher. The thought of going up to her and asking her these questions is so outlandish that I might as well consider flying to space to enjoy a Happy Meal with Han Solo and Luke Skywalker.

Cynthia reminds me of a character from *The Cosby Show* spin-off, *A Different World*, which details the shenanigans of the young Denise Huxtable and her group of wayward pals at the mostly black Hillman College. Cynthia is the same as the mouthy Jaleesa Vinson Tyler. Thank God for Hollywood movies or television. Without them, I'd be lost. And they tell you this stuff rots your brain.

I'm by my locker, looking down the hallway at Cynthia and her posse. I've grown to hate my winter jacket. I can tell that it is dangerously unhip. My boots make me look like a special-needs snowman; I clomp around the halls like it's my first day on the moon. No one else wears acid-washed jeans, but they are used as the punchline in jokes on *Letterman*. My sweaters are gaily colourful, but all the kids wear black. It's as if I've shown up to a funeral dressed as a clown.

Everyone at Hillman College wore colourful sweaters. Maybe TV *is* bad for you. Clearly, it's done nothing for my fashion sense.

"You new here?" asks a voice behind me.

I turn around, startled. "Ja. How did you know?"

"Number one—your locker. No pictures." I look at the naked, battered steel of my locker and compare it to my neighbour's frenzied collage. "Number two," says my neighbour, "your accent."

Oh, right. My accent. It's so thick with a Johannesburg drawl that when I go to the convenience store and ask for a Sprite, it comes out "Spraaaaaght." It's as gentle as a brick covered in sandpaper bashed repeatedly against the ears. I've been speaking English my entire life, yet here I am barely intelligible. *The Twilight Zone* redux.

My neighbour is small, with too-big glasses perched on his nose. At school in South Africa, I would have turned him upside down, dumped him in a garbage can, and called him a nerd. Believe it or not, under my Smarties upchuck sweater, I have big muscles. That doesn't seem to count for much around these parts. But in Johannesburg, it kept me from being turned upside down and dumped in a garbage can.

My small neighbour takes in the direction of my gaze. He sees that I am looking at Cynthia. She is laughing at something one of her friends has said, her braids flying like weapons in a ninja movie.

"Her? Cynthia?" says the little guy. "Forget it, man. You don't stand a chance. She's cool, but she has, like, twelve boyfriends. I'm just telling you this 'cause you're new."

It takes a long time for me to turn my head toward the boy with the big glasses. For the duration of the head turn, I'm thinking about the fact that he considers it to be perfectly normal—absolutely A-OK—for me to lust after a black girl. Does he not realize that such a thing could not possibly have crossed my mind? Where does he think I'm from? How does he think the world works?

"I have a girlfriend," I lie.

He nods. "Sure. Of course. Sorry for the mistake."

I let the sarcasm bubble around us for moment. Then I shut my locker and walk away.

I sit in the basement of our new home and watch *Cheers*. It feels safe in the basement. Unconfusing. And North American: there are no basements in South African homes because, my father tells me, the ground never freezes so the foundations need not be so deep. I watch three episodes of *Cheers* in a row. I laugh. Then I remember something I read a day or so ago.

Ted Danson—who plays Sam, the owner of the Boston drinking hole—is dating Whoopie Goldberg in real life. A white man and a black woman. It seemed absurd to me when I first read it. An aberration. A piece of Hollywood gossip that didn't really square with reality. Some sort of stunt. Could Danson and Goldberg really go steady? Share a milkshake with two straws? Sleep together?

Which makes me think of Whitney Houston.

I love Whitney Houston. I have a copy of her sophomore record *Whitney* buried in my stack of CDs. She wears a white tank top that struggles with the bounty of her chest, and she stares out at me, and me alone. You want to argue that the music is crap, go ahead. But you cannot argue with that tank top.

Once, at school in Johannesburg, I made the mistake of mentioning my lust for Whitney Houston to one of my school friends. Initially, this was met with laughter. Then derision. "Kaffir lover," my friends called me. *Kaffir* is a bad word for a black person. I was too big to be dumped upside down in a garbage can. But I was not too big to be reminded of how the world works. Separation. Apartheid.

Did my interest in Whitney Houston somehow link to my interest in Cynthia? Was my little locker neighbour on the money?

There is no furniture in our house. It has yet to arrive in a ship container from South Africa. So I sit on a box and watch TV. And watch *Cheers*.

My removal from the Claude Watson School for the Arts is abrupt. On my seventh day, my mother tells me that everyone agrees it would be best if I transfer to a school closer to home, with an arts program less—as they put it—"outside your realm of experience." Perhaps the art teacher was terrified by my mannequin. Or the math teacher by my walkouts. Or the librarian by my eating among her dusty books.

My little neighbour says nothing as I clear out my locker. It's as if he knew I wouldn't last. I stare down the hallway at Cynthia and her pals. They carry on as if nothing is wrong. Their lives are set. They will move forward with no complications. I feel a surge of bitterness. *In my old world*, I think, I would have been the boss of you people. But the thought feels small, the bitterness has no bite. They are not locked in here with me, I now realize. I am locked up in here with them.

The crown that is the birthright of the white male in South Africa has been removed from my head. You'd think I'd miss it. But no. I think I might feel like Superman must have right before he flew for the first time: a sense of lightness, a tingling in the legs, a surge in the heart.

I take my eye off the black girl, and walk toward the doors and out into the snow.

A week or so later. A small, concrete plaza in a sea of asphalt parking bays. Three of us stand hidden from the wind in a maze of hallways behind the Shoppers Drug Mart, where I am employed as a part-time merchandiser. It is my first job. I am to come here twice a week after school, and every Sunday.

"Where the fuck," asks the black dude, "on planet earth did you get that jacket?"

"Nowhere."

This is the first conversation I've ever had with a black person roughly my own age. And I'm not coming out so good.

"Man, that is some retro shit. It's out of *Electric Boogaloo*."

Despite myself, I smile. The black dude, name of Lairie, runs the floor. He is three years older than me, wears a Boston Red Sox cap backwards, and wants to be a rapper. He sort of looks like T.C., the helicopter pilot from *Magnum P.I.*, which makes me like him even if he is being a bit of a dick.

"I lay some cardboard down, you'll breakdance for us?" asks Lairie.

"Leave him alone," says a skinny white kid named Ian. "He's fresh off the South African boat. He'll skin you alive."

I go red, but Lairie and Ian just laugh.

"Damn," says Lairie, "I better behave."

After work, it snows like damnation. Ian insists we go for a coffee. We sit together, and Lairie lectures me on rap. "What you listen to is not real. The Beastie Boys are fine, but they make you feel safe, because you're a crazed, bedsheet-wearing white supremacist." Ian laughs. "But thing is, you *ain't* safe. You need to spread your horizons."

Spread them where? How far? How much do I have to learn in this new place? And at that moment—with movie melodrama timing—Cynthia walks into the coffee shop. She looks down at me, and through me. It's been over a week since I left the school, and she doesn't remember me. She is with an Asian boy. They hold hands.

Suddenly I realize that I am like that man in the *Twilight Zone* episode. I am reading a nursery book and learning anew. Lairie is still speaking to me about rap. He hands me a CD. Black Sheep. I take it from him. He extends a hand to shake, and says, "So you'll listen, yeah. We got a deal." His hand feels rough in mine, worked.

As we shake, I think I might be getting the hang of the nursery book.

Shadow Play

RUI UMEZAWA

My father was a theoretical physicist whose mind was occupied most times with intricate movements of subatomic particles. When I was born, he was still teaching at the prestigious Tokyo University in Japan, but he yearned to conduct research outside the country, where he knew there would be more academic freedom. He followed career opportunities first to France, then later Italy, the States, and finally Canada, and his family dragged their feet behind him. In the mid-seventies, we moved to Edmonton, but for the nine years previous, I grew up in the American Midwest in a city called Milwaukee, Wisconsin.

Milwaukee at the time was the setting for a television show called *Happy Days*, which fondly recalled American life in the fifties. A similar sitcom twenty years later—*That '70s Show*, also set in Milwaukee—would fondly recall American life in the seventies. The quintessence of American life was not New York or California but the middle of the United States. When Americans thought of more innocent times, they pictured suburbs with old, sturdy houses and neatly trimmed lawns, typical of Milwaukee, Wisconsin.

Rain never falls in my memories of going to school there. I recall running track in a grey T-shirt and red shorts, skinny arms flailing in the sun. I recall spraining my middle finger trying to catch a football, which nonetheless slipped through my hands. I recall coming to bat with a man on first then hitting a grounder to shortstop, resulting in a picture-perfect double play against my team. I recall streams of swear words falling from Brian McArthur's mouth. Whenever I struck out, he would kick at the dirt and say the same thing:

"Swing and a miss, baby! Swing and a miss!"

Brian was a big kid with a big voice and sinewy forearms and legs. We had known each other since the third grade. His pet name for me was Ragu. He was at once my tormentor and my friend. Every December, he reminded me of Japan's invasion of Pearl Harbor by throwing me against a wall, but he also taught me how to shoot hoops and swing a bat. Like much of my life then, Brian was a terrifying enigma.

Our house in Milwaukee was old and majestic. My bedroom overlooked Maryland Avenue, lined with ancient trees that formed a lush, leafy canopy in the summertime. Through their gnarled limbs, I could see the driveway of our neighbours across the street. Their daughter Kirsten, who was my age, worked on her tennis swing every day, slamming a citrus-green ball against their garage. Whether she was any good, I had no idea, but her legs were always tanned each year by June. I had just started to understand that I could starve for something other than food.

About half a block down my side of the street was Leslie's house. When we first moved to the neighbourhood, Leslie often came to our door and invited me out to play. One year, she wore an orthopaedic brace around her neck to straighten her spine. The same year, I sent away for some mail-order novelty items, including a pack of hot garlic gum. I tricked Leslie into trying a piece on our way home from school. She gagged and, unable to bend over, threw up on the front of her sweater. She stopped coming over after that.

"Swing and a miss, baby!"

A mile farther down Maryland Avenue lived Julie, who sat next to me in math during our sophomore year in high school. She sat with her legs crossed, absent-mindedly combing her blonde hair with her fingers. Julie was fond of short skirts. I was fond of Julie's short skirts. Our teacher, Mr. Andersen, often caught me in a stupor because of Julie's skirts. Once, when I could not answer one of his questions, he put his massive hand behind my head and pulled my face to his. "I thought *you guys* were supposed to be good at math." Mr. Anderson did not so much speak as bark. He also coached football. I knew exactly what he meant, but nonetheless had no idea who "we guys" were. The only other Asian in our school was a Chinese kid in the grade above mine, who seemed every bit as bewildered as I.

So who were we, and who were we supposed to be? There were countless cool white people on television. They were secret agents and police detectives and superheroes and cowboys. They jumped into cars without opening doors, flew through the air, wore Stetsons, and fired guns at things they did not like. There were also cool black people, and even Hispanics, but virtually no cool Asians.

Asian characters in movies and on television, especially the important ones, were often played by white actors. Kwai Chang Caine, the Shaolin Buddhist monk who wandered the American Old West in the popular TV show *Kung Fu*, was played by a pale, skinny guy whose idea of Eastern wisdom was to utter inaudible and incomprehensible metaphors. Caine was so obtuse, you couldn't help sympathizing with his racist tormenters, who inevitably were flattened by his martial arts prowess before each episode ended.

Still, I wondered if people might not like me more if I dispensed poetic insights as readily as Caine. "The flower petal falls as gracefully as the snowflake," I told Julie when she asked me whether the sine of an angle is the ratio of its adjacent side or the opposite side to the hypotenuse.

"If you don't know, just fucking say so," she said before turning to the guy behind her.

"Swing and a miss, baby! Swing and a miss!"

Because of Kwai Chang Caine, I was frequently asked whether I studied the martial arts. Things would have been easier had the answer been a simple no, but my professorial father had taught me what he claimed were judo techniques. They consisted mostly of taking one's opponent by the shoulders, sneaking your leg behind his, and tripping him. There were a few variations, but they always ended with tripping. No one at school was terribly impressed.

My lack of skills in the martial arts later became more conspicuous because of Bruce Lee. Bruce (I always thought of him by his first name) was the first cool Asian I had encountered outside of the manga magazines my relatives sent me from Japan. His characters were always handsome but bashful, except when they flew into manic, berserk rages with the elegance of a ballet dancer.

"Fists of fury, baby!"

Brian McArthur, who had been fanatical about professional wrestling in elementary school, suddenly became obsessed with martial arts films. He made sounds like a castrated cat as he rapidly fired punches that stopped an inch from my face.

That both Bruce Lee and Kwai Chang Caine were Chinese did not stop me from claiming them as role models. This seemed only fair considering I was called Chink more often than Jap or

Nip. But Bruce never grew old. He died accidentally at the peak of his popularity, eternally charismatic and graceful. I was about as charismatic and graceful as a barstool with uneven legs.

I listened to Black Sabbath and Dave Brubeck, as well as Dvořák and the Partridge Family, which meant everyone had reason to disdain my taste in music. I pinned posters of fluorescent peace signs on my wall and lit them with my black-light desk lamp. After an evening of watching Kirsten practise tennis on her driveway, I lay on my bed and stared at purple shadows swimming on my ceiling.

Sunlight flooded the gymnasium the day we met Mr. Shober, whose wrists were as thick as my thighs. His jaw was a chiselled block of granite. He wore shirts two sizes too small. His voice was godlike when he called us "gentlemen."

"Thirty push-ups, gentlemen!" he barked whenever the mood struck him. We collapsed in unison and flopped on our bellies like suffocating fish.

Whenever reality became too intense, my mind fled to Bruce Lee movies, American television shows, or Japanese manga. Gasping and grunting while face down on the floor, I recalled how, in *The Star of the Giants*, a diminutive high school dropout beat impossible odds to become the ace pitcher for Japan's most popular baseball team. Other Japanese comic-book heroes similarly small of stature subjected themselves to torturous training to become boxing champions, karate masters, and superhuman volleyball players.

I had forgotten to breathe and felt my skull engorge with blood in search of oxygen. I could not possibly do thirty push-ups—my triceps had dissolved after twenty. But in honour of melodrama, I decided to die trying. Mechanically dropping my chest to lift it back up, I arched my spine when my abs surrendered and crushed a scream between my back molars.

Mr. Shober abruptly stopped us and called me to the front of the class. "Let me shake your hand," he said. "That is *precisely* what I mean by effort."

Without releasing his grip, he looked down his nose at the rest of the class. "Thirty more, gentlemen!" he shouted.

Praise, especially for such trivial activity, was perplexing. Athleticism and sports—with the exception of Olympic events in which Japan participated—received little attention from my parents. Science and music were considered the highest of human pursuits. Among the manga from Japan was also the story of Beethoven enduring his father's strictest training to become the most esteemed composer in history. My mother emulated his father's teaching methods, and practising the piano meant being beaten with a ruler if I did not learn fast enough.

Flawless performances at recitals were expected, not extraordinary. Similarly, receiving the highest marks in all my subjects (except phys. ed.) was just another opportunity to remind me that my achievements meant nothing unless they were repeated every semester of every year until I graduated with a Ph.D. from an Ivy League university.

So I quietly delighted in receiving praise for being the symbol of perseverance in Mr. Shober's class. The role also came with an unexpected advantage. Whenever I tired of push-ups or running laps, all I need do was quash my face in agony before collapsing like a spent lover.

"Good effort!" Mr. Shober, without fail, gave me a thumbs-up. He scorned others who quit without obvious suffering.

Acting skills disguised as diligence compensated for my lack of coordination in gym class until the wrestling unit started. Dissatisfied with my father's "judo techniques," I had faithfully watched *All-Star Wrestling* every day after school. Osmosis was the only explanation as to why, of all sports, I actually happened to be good at wrestling.

I intuitively sidestepped opponents' attacks before they were launched, just as Édouard "The Flying Frenchman" Carpentier evaded "Killer" Kowalski and sent him into the ropes. My lanky arms looped around my opponent with a mind of their own when executing a textbook double-leg takedown. Mr. Shober finally praised me for something other than effort. I was, however, dismayed to learn that familiar techniques such as the Flying Neckbreaker and the Claw were disallowed.

Endearingly predictable, Mr. Shober convinced me to join the wrestling team. The idea that I could be an athlete was remarkably foreign. Our coach, Mr. Warren, was new to the school. Standing barely over five feet, he was as short as my Japanese comic-book heroes. His iron will was also as formidable as theirs. I never imagined I could sweat so much. The dehydration combined with the endorphin euphoria was nothing short of bewildering after practice. After a few weeks, I pleasantly discovered I could do *more* than thirty push-ups. I was hardly winded after running. I opened mayonnaise jars with ease. I was invincible.

I returned home every night just in time for dinner, incredibly hungry and thirsty. My parents never asked how I might be enjoying my new-found pursuit. They had received news of my joining the wrestling team only with mild apprehension.

"Don't let it affect your studies," my father said.

"Or your piano practice," my mother added.

"If you find it's too much, just quit. You have more important things to do."

My parents did not come to my first and only match at a neighbouring school, a twenty-minute bus ride away. Joining the team had done nothing to endear me to the real jocks, the hulkish columns of muscle who also joined other sports teams and were the most popular kids in the school. They ignored me and my teammates from the lighter weight divisions as we sat at the back of the bus. Despite their athleticism, most of these dwarfish wrestlers were clearly more comfortable in math class or buried in a novel. One of them was my lab partner in chemistry.

We sat together again while waiting our turns to enter the ring. The vastness of an unfamiliar, crowded gymnasium, the palpable masculine tension, and the uncertainty of pitting my skills against a stranger's were novel and exciting. Bone and muscle slammed against each other and against the mat. Shrill whistles cut the pungent air. Coaches shouted instructions, pretending to be in control still.

My opponent was about six inches shorter than I, but his compact frame only meant greater muscle mass. Had he been Asian, he would have resembled Bruce Lee. I *was* Asian but could never look like Bruce. My long arms, however, proved advantageous again when, at the start of the match, I circled to his right then lunged at his left leg. Pushing against his hip with my head, I pulled his leg from beneath him, and we both fell onto the mat in a heap.

I would never forget this small but exhilarating victory of scoring the first takedown. I also would always remember how, in the next instant, my opponent expertly tipped my balance so I would roll over his shoulder. I struggled to regain the advantage, but he circumvented my every move as if he had seen it countless times. Bridging my back and straining my neck against his weight, I felt an eternity pass in the minute it took for him to pin me.

My teammates looked at me sadly as I exited the ring. "Tough break, man," one of them said. I gave him five.

Mr. Warren came over and shook my hand.

"Nice try," he said. He pointed with his chin toward my opponent. "He's got a couple years on you in experience. Don't let it get you down." As he walked away, I realized Mr. Warren must have been one of the smallest wrestlers on his team when he competed. We would have sat at the back of the bus together.

Because I had been ignored much of the time at school, I assumed no one ever talked about me in my absence. Someone, however, had mentioned to Leslie that I'd joined the wrestling team. Sunbeams fell across her shoulders like curtains one Saturday afternoon when she and Kirsten stopped to talk to me outside our neighbourhood pharmacy. By this time Leslie was through with her orthopaedic brace, and her smile shimmered like morning dew. We had not spoken for a long time.

"Is it true?" she asked, excited.

"Yeah." I could not understand why she might be interested, and I was suspicious.

"That's far out. I should come and watch you sometime."

"Okay." I felt at once hungry and nauseated.

I glanced at Kirsten. She looked away as if acknowledging that my presence might oblige her to cross the street and spend time with me between tennis practices. A week earlier, a few of us had found her passed out on the sidewalk after a school dance. Speculating on what she might have ingested had been the centre of much gossip since then. I did not understand that she was too busy fighting her own demons to consider mine. I imagined her bare legs beneath her jeans.

The moment shattered when I was shoved from behind. "*Five Fingers of Death, baby!*"

As athletic as Brian McArthur clearly was, he did not join sports teams. He and a few others like him had an edge different from jocks, and sharper. They did not wear lettermen jackets. The cars they drove were dilapidated. They worked after school rather than attend football practice. This did not mean his presence was any less imposing. Something cold gripped my stomach despite the sunny afternoon when he emerged from the corner store.

"Ragu!" I winced when he called me by his pet name. "How's wrestling? You should be doing kung fu instead, tough guy!"

It was impossible to tell whether he himself studied martial arts or was simply mimicking what he saw in the movies. Whichever the case, he at first appeared to know what he was doing as he fired more punches, this time at my abdomen. Then one actually connected. My body collapsed in an instant, dropping in a perfect vertical line onto the sidewalk.

"What are you doing?" Leslie shrieked somewhere above me.

"Hey, I didn't mean that."

I lay still, feeling the gritty concrete against my face. I was not badly hurt. Regaining my breath was not terribly difficult. Getting up, however, was. I knew Brian had meant no harm. By standing up and dusting myself off, I could make this embarrassing moment disappear for both of us. But I did not want to.

Instead, I let the familiar warmth behind my eyes blossom. I wanted the world to stop, and when it didn't, I sank into self-pity. I thought about home and about school, and for the life of me, nothing at that moment made any sense. I no longer wanted to put up with this shit. I no longer wanted to be called Jap or Nip or Chink. I no longer wanted to be associated with karate or thick accents or confusing mysticism. I simply did not know how to make it all go away, and I did not know how to stop crying.

"Sorry, man," Brian apologized tenderly as he helped me to my feet.

Words to pardon him did not make it past my trembling lips. Unable to say anything coherent, I hobbled away—toward

school, because going home meant walking with Leslie and
Kirsten.

"Swing and a miss, baby! Swing and a miss!"

I quit wrestling the following week. Mr. Warren betrayed only
a moment of surprise. Half the guys who had started were no
longer showing up for practice anyway. He appeared too weary
to argue as he told me to return my equipment. Mr. Shober, on
the other hand, could not have been more shocked had I turned
into a cow.

"Are you sure?" he asked when I told him at the start of gym
class. I nodded. His surprise turned quickly to what looked like
hurt.

"Why?"

I pushed the knife in deeper. "Because I hate practice."

He raised an eyebrow.

"And I have to study," I added.

Determined to make this a teachable moment, he shook his
head and rested a hand on my shoulder. "You know," he said,
"people admire real accomplishments precisely because they're
hard to achieve."

"I know." I shrugged. "Can I go, please?"

"What are you going to do now?"

The question was reasonable but sounded odd to me. Who
cared what I was going to do when I did not even know who I was?
Self-motivation was difficult without a sense of self. There was
no one for me to be except Kwai Chang Caine or Bruce or
someone I'd read about in manga. There was nothing more to
life than what I saw on television. I didn't even understand that
if a girl did not like me, she simply did not like me—and that this
had nothing to do with my not being a letterman or a superhero.

Mr. Shober and I continued our charade during phys. ed. I
continued to pretend to try my best, and he kept giving me a

thumbs-up. Kirsten kept practising tennis. Brian saw every kung fu movie that hit theatres. Julie ignored me in math class. Even in these pathetic memories of Milwaukee, Wisconsin, the sun never stops shining, making the shadows all the more stark.

The Airplane Overhead

EVA WISEMAN

I am sitting beside my husband on the front seat of our rental car at the Hungarian border. A long line of vehicles snakes behind us. A guard, in a watchtower on the side of the road, has his binoculars focused on us. My heart begins a rat-a-tat dance in my throat, and I clutch my husband's arm. Twenty-year-old memories crowd my brain.

"What's the matter with you?" Nathan asks.

"I keep thinking of the last time I crossed this border when I was a kid."

Nathan smiles. He has heard the same story a thousand times.

"You have nothing to worry about. They need tourists like us."

I remove with trembling hands my passport from the outside pocket of my purse and leaf to the page with the Hungarian stamp on it. It says: LEFT HUNGARY ILLEGALLY. I put it back in my purse.

"It was a good visit, but it'll be great to be home," Nathan says. "I miss the kids."

"I do too."

I desperately want to hug my children and to discover how they have broken every one of my rules while I was visiting my native land for the first time since my family escaped from Hungary during the Hungarian Revolution. I was only nine years old when we crossed the border into Austria one dark November night in 1956, as the Communist regime temporarily lost its grip on the country. I remember holding my mother's hand, the long, long line of refugees, and the rocky terrain that caused me to stumble and skin my knees.

I am torn. A deep desire to be gone from this border, with its barricades and armed soldiers, overwhelms me. I want to be back in Winnipeg, back to my old routine. I want to go grocery shopping at the Dominion at the end of my street, and meet my mother at the chocolate shop on Saturday afternoons for coffee and pastry. Yet, at the same time, I don't want to leave Hungary. I feel that in leaving my native country, I will be leaving an essential piece of myself behind.

"It's never easy to leave home," I tell Nathan, waving my hand in the direction of the barricade manned by armed soldiers.

"What are you talking about? You don't belong here! Canada is your home."

A border guard walks along the endless row of cars, stopping beside each one.

"I wish he would hurry up," Nathan says. "We have to return the car in Austria by five o'clock this afternoon."

The guard reaches our vehicle and peers through the window. I shrink from his intrusive gaze, but there is nowhere to hide. The man's cold eyes sweep over me. I clutch my hands together. I don't want to give him the satisfaction of seeing them shaking.

Rewind Twenty-One Years:
Winnipeg, Elementary School, 1957

I followed the principal as closely as my short legs would allow, but she was walking so rapidly that I had trouble keeping up with her. She stopped in front of a door at the end of the hall with a sign that read GRADE FOUR. She patted me on the shoulder before knocking.

A roomful of eyes stared at me. Somebody snickered in the back of the room, but I couldn't tell who it was, for my oxfords drew my eyes like a magnet. How scuffed they were! The principal was talking to the class. I heard my name but couldn't understand a single word of what she was saying. The teacher led me to a desk at the front of the room. I kept my head down but couldn't resist a sideward glance at the girl sitting at the desk next to mine. She stuck out her tongue when she saw me looking at her.

The bell rang, and all the kids marched out of the room into the schoolyard. The teacher took me by the hand, and we followed them. A large rectangle had been drawn with white paint in the middle of the yard. The students from the class were clustered around it. The teacher said something to me and left. A boy with red hair, holding a large bat and a white ball, and a girl with a blonde ponytail called out the names of different students, who went to stand beside whoever had called them. Everybody ignored me. All the kids' names were said, until I was the only one left. The red-headed boy and the girl with the ponytail seemed to be arguing with each other. They pointed at me repeatedly. I heard the word *baseball* several times, but I didn't understand what they were saying. Finally, the boy waved his arm and beckoned me to follow him. He led me to the white square and pressed the bat into my hands. Another boy took the ball from him.

Before I knew what was happening, the second boy threw the ball in my direction with all his might. I dropped to my knees and shielded my face with my hands. The ball grazed my elbow, and I fell in the dirt, tearing my stockings.

"Dummy!" one of the kids said.

Everybody around me began to laugh. *He must have said something funny*, I said to myself.

"Dummmy! Dummmy!" I repeated, the fat sounds rolling off my tongue awkwardly.

The kids from the class surrounded me.

"Dummy! Dummy!" they screamed.

Somebody tugged on my pigtails really hard. I couldn't stop the tears rolling from my eyes. I asked them why they were being so mean, but they laughed even harder at my Hungarian.

The bell rang. A teacher appeared. Everybody lined up in front of the door and filed into the school. The teacher motioned for me to follow them, before she too went inside. I couldn't move. I was rooted to the ground. It was so silent in the yard that I could hear the chirping of a cricket and my own ragged breathing.

An airplane overhead shattered the silence. It cut a wide, white swath in the blue sky. It was flying so low that I could even see its propellers. A deep desire to be on it overwhelmed me. I wanted the plane to carry me back to my beloved old school in Hungary. I wanted that plane to take me back to my friends, with whom I would jump rope while singing merry tunes. My heart swelled with desire to be on that plane and return on it to all that was familiar and loved. The noise of the plane grew fainter and fainter. I wiped away my tears and headed for the school door.

Fast-Forward Four Years:
Winnipeg, Junior High School, 1961

The lighting was poor in the girls' washroom. I leaned close to the mirror to see my reflection and smoothed down a lock of my hair. No matter how much I teased my hair or how much hairspray I used, it was too curly for a perfect beehive.

Next, I went into a cubicle to slip on the white mohair sweater I had stolen from Mama's dresser. Mama wouldn't lend it to me after I had tried it on for her.

"There is no way you'll leave this house dressed like that!" she cried. "It makes you look like a little *Kurveh!*"

"I am not a whore!" I yelled back.

Mama was so old-fashioned. She still wanted me to wear childish clothes, as I used to in Hungary. She didn't realize that this was how all the popular girls dressed in Canada. She left me no choice—I borrowed the sweater without her permission and put it in my satchel while she was at work.

I opened the door of the cubicle a crack and peeked out to make sure no one was about before I went back to the mirror. I turned sideways to get the full effect of the sweater. It was tight in the right places. My navy skirt was getting shiny from all the washings and ironings, but hopefully nobody would notice it, not with the groovy sweater I was wearing. I twirled in front of the mirror. I thought that when I half closed my eyes I looked a little like the movie star Annette Funicello. Finally, I put on some of the pink lipstick I kept hidden in my pencil case. I felt bad about deceiving Mama, but she made me wipe it off whenever she saw it on my lips. It was no use complaining to Papa. He was even more strict than Mama.

The gym looked like a nightclub in the dim lighting. Balloons hung from the ceiling, and crepe paper crinkled on the walls. It took me a minute to orient myself. Anita Writeman and the other popular girls were standing around the punch bowl while the kids nobody wanted to be seen with stood at the other end of the long table.

None of the foxy girls looked in my direction as I set out toward their group. From the corner of my eye, I saw gangly Hilda Weisz, surrounded by the rest of the undesirables, waving to me. Our parents were good friends, and I saw Hilda almost every weekend when our families visited each other. I had to come up with a million excuses to discourage her from coming with me to our grade eight class's sock hop.

"Please, God, please, God, let her leave me alone!" I prayed under my breath. No such luck. She rushed up to me.

"I was wondeering wheen you-u-ud be here," she stuttered earnestly. "Leet's da-a-ance!" Her accent could be heard over her stammer. For a moment, I remembered being taunted, "Dummy! Dummy!" in the schoolyard when I'd arrived in Canada.

Hilda held out her hand. My expression must have given me away. She blushed beet red and backed away, muttering to herself. I opened my mouth to call her back, but before I could speak somebody touched my arm. It was Anita Writeman. Rose Craven, her shadow, was standing behind her.

Anita pointed in Hilda's direction. "Is she a friend of yours?"

I blinked, but she didn't disappear. Anita Writeman was actually talking to me! There were two kinds of girls in our school. The first type, like me, walked to school even on the coldest of winter days freezing the top part of our thighs left bare by our nylons. Most often, our families had immigrated to Canada from countries like Hungary or Poland. Our parents spoke English with a heavy Eastern European accent, if they spoke it at all. The second group of girls were those who passed us in fancy cars driven by their fathers dressed in fancy suits, honking their horns as they went by. These girls' families had settled in Canada generations ago. Their parents spoke English without an accent. Nor did they have to act as translators when their parents went to see the doctor or had business dealings with the bank. Anita Writeman definitely belonged to this second group.

Anita was the most popular girl in our grade. She was not only the president of our class but also the president of the B'Nai Brith Youth Organization chapter all the Jewish girls belonged to. Mama tortured me so much about making some Jewish friends that I finally caved in and decided to become a member of the BBYO. I told Rose Craven, the secretary of the chapter, that I wanted to join. Rose said that the executive of their chapter would vote on my application at their next meeting. I tried not to get my hopes up, but at least Rose didn't turn me down outright. I was surprised by her friendliness, for she was usually quite nasty to me. I never understood why she disliked me so.

"Are you friends?" Anita repeated, nodding her head toward Hilda.

"I barely know her. She is in some of my classes." The words coming out of my mouth horrified me, but there was nothing I could do to take them back.

Anita turned to Rose. "I told you she wouldn't be friends with such a freak!" She threw her arms up in the air. "Let's dance!" she said and began to twist. I didn't have any trouble keeping up with her, thanks to all the practising Hilda and I had done in front of the mirror in my room.

The night passed in a haze of fun and laughter. After a while, I didn't even notice Hilda's accusing eyes. The boys stayed at the far end of the gym, and the girls danced with each other. I noticed the blond brush cut of Neil Schwarz towering over his neighbours in the boys' group. As far as I was concerned, Neil was the cutest boy not only in our class but in the entire school. How I wished he knew that I was alive!

I was out of breath by the time the teachers placed tall bottles of Coke on the table in a straight line like soldiers on a battle-field. They set bowls of potato chips beside the drinks. Once again, the girls crowded around the table, but the boys approached it more cautiously. Neil stopped in front of me.

"Hi," he said.

I stared at him like an idiot, unable to find the right words.

"Good party," he said.

"Yes," I managed to croak.

"I'll get you a Coke."

"Sure," was my brilliant answer.

He leaned closer. "I didn't know that you and Anita Writeman were friends."

"Well ... sort of ..."

"What do you mean?"

"Yes, we're friends."

"Oh no we're not!" shouted a loud voice behind us.

I spun around and almost bumped into Rose Craven. Anita was standing beside her, a furious expression on her face.

"How dare you to try to push yourself into our crowd? Who do you think you are?" she spluttered. "You were right, Rose," she said. "Give an immigrant an inch and she'll take a mile!" Her eyes swept over me coldly before she turned to Neil. The sudden change in her expression was comical. She smiled at him flirtatiously.

"Why are you bothering with this DP?" she asked him. She tapped Rose's arm. "Let's go!" she ordered, and turned on her heels and flounced away before Neil could answer her. Rose followed her more sedately, but not before throwing me a malicious look.

The room began to whirl. What had I done? I grasped the edge of the table to steady myself. By the time the room came to a standstill, Anita and Rose were at the other end of the gym. Neil was still beside me, his eyes full of pity.

"Well, I've got to go," he said to the wooden floor.

"Me too."

I held my head high, my back straight, my tears in check as I marched out of the gym.

The next morning, I made sure that I slipped into my homeroom just before the bell, for I didn't want anybody to talk to me about the dance. Our teacher, Mrs. Willis, was hot on my heels. As I sank into my desk, I saw Rose, a sly look on her face, whisper in Anita's ear. I also saw Neil glance at me and then become so deeply absorbed in the book in front of him that he appeared oblivious to his surroundings.

Mrs. Willis began to drone on about William Shakespeare. Not a single word of her lesson penetrated my ears. She had the annoying habit of interrupting her lecture and pointing her ruler at a student to ask a question. Before long, her ruler was aimed toward me. However, after a quick look at my face, she muttered, "Perhaps not!" and moved on to a boy in the next row.

The bell rang, and I dawdled while the rest of the students stampeded to the door like a herd of cattle. All the kids were gone, except Rose Craven. She sidled up to my desk.

"Hi," she said. Her smile sent shivers down my back.

I didn't answer but continued gathering up my books as quickly as possible.

"I've got some news for you."

"I don't want to talk to you."

She laughed. "You'll want to hear this. I told Anita that you want to join our chapter. She said that she'd resign as president if we let you in. Nobody wants her to quit. So I think it would be useless to have the executive vote." She leaned closer, showering me with her spittle. "Face it! Nobody wants you!" Then she was gone.

The cool fall air ruffled my hair as I set out for home.

"Nobody wants me. Nobody wants me," was the song of the dead leaves crunching under my feet.

"Nobody wants me. Nobody wants me," was the rhythm made by my shoes on the cracked pavement.

The roar of an airplane overhead drowned out my thoughts. I immediately yearned to be on that plane, to be anywhere else but on this street, with its barren trees. I wasn't paying attention to the potholes in the sidewalk, so I stumbled and fell to the ground, ripping my nylons. For an instant, I was, once again, back on the baseball field in the schoolyard four years ago. However, the pain in my knees brought me back to reality. I tried to pull together the edges of the tears in my nylons, but they were beyond salvage. "There goes my babysitting money," I muttered.

"They don't want me ... to hell with them! If they don't want me, I don't want them—ever!" I cried to the naked trees. "Never again will I humiliate myself in front of them!"

And I didn't—not when I walked to school alone, not when I refused to share the smallest piece of myself with anybody who made overtures of friendship, not when I ate lunch by myself, not when I buried my nose in a book on a Saturday night. My loneliness didn't bother me, for I knew as well as I knew my own name that I didn't belong in this school, in this city, in this country. My real life was somewhere else, waiting to begin, waiting for me to live it.

Fast-Forward Seventeen Years:
The Hungarian Border, 1978

The border guard sticks his hand into the car.

"*Utlevelek!* Passports!" he translates in heavily accented English.

Nathan pulls his passport out of his shirt pocket and hands it over. I remove mine from my purse once again and give it to him.

The guard examines Nathan's passport and returns it. It's my turn next. I see him flip to the visa page. He glances up and looks me in the eye. I look back at him, unblinking, for a moment as long as eternity. Never would he guess the racing of my heart or the clammy fear in my stomach. He hands back my passport and waves us toward the barricade. It goes up. Our car speeds up. We're in Austria. I can breathe again.

Fast-Forward Twelve Hours: An Airplane, Ten Thousand Feet Above Toronto

"We're beginning our final approach to Toronto," announces the flight attendant. "Your seatbelts should be locked and your chairs put into upright position with your trays up. All hand luggage should be stowed under the seat in front of you."

I lean back in my seat, close my eyes, and remember all the familiar places in Hungary that I have shown to my husband— my old home, the playground with my favourite swing, and the school I used to attend. I say goodbye to them all, together with my childhood self, for my life is now somewhere else.

Nathan reaches over my seat. My eyes fly open. He pulls up the blind covering the window next to my shoulder.

"Look," he says, "how beautiful!"

The lights of Toronto glimmer in the darkness below us.

I press my nose against the cold window. The airplane lowers its altitude. We are going to land very soon. My ears pop and my heart soars with joy. I am going home. I am Canadian.

Permission
to Work

TING-XING YE

I got off the plane in Toronto on a hot August afternoon, trembling with excitement and anticipating the start of another chapter in my turbulent life. But I had no idea of what was in store for me in this vastly different country. It was 1987, and I had been invited by Toronto's York University to be a visiting scholar in English literature. I looked around and sighed with relief as I realized that the dream I thought I had lost forever on a horrible night over twenty years earlier might come true. I might be able to take charge of my life after all.

I was fourteen when a gang of Red Guards burst into our home on Purple Sunshine Lane in downtown Shanghai, shouting threats and political slogans. Both of my parents were dead, and there was no one to protect my brothers, my sisters, and me. The guards screamed insults at us because our father had been a business owner. They said that we had our father's "black capitalist blood" in our veins, and therefore, we were enemies of the beloved Communist motherland.

Claiming to look for "forbidden materials" like books, music recordings, and paintings, when they were really after money and valuable objects to carry off and sell, they ransacked our apartment. But we had been living in poverty for years, so the guards came up empty-handed and furious. They turned violent, pushing and slapping my siblings and me around, smashing dishes, and kicking over our few sticks of furniture. They left in a temper, moving on to their next victims and leaving the five of us shaking with fear and despair.

It was 1966. Political turmoil and unrest were raging across China. If I had ever nurtured the idea that I might someday have control over my life, I lost it that night.

Two years later, when I turned sixteen, I was informed by the Party Secretary in my school that I was to be sent to a "reform through labour" farm far north of Shanghai, as a part of the government program to re-educate youth.

My exile was for life.

Until then, the farm had been populated by prisoners. Its alkaline soil was good only for growing cotton, but I and hundreds of other teens were ordered to convert the fields into rice paddies. Year after year, our swollen hands and aching backs from bending over double were our only reward for a vain effort to coax grain from the stubborn soil.

After six years' labour on the farm, and in one of the ironic twists of fate that were to mark my life, I was given an opportunity to write a university entrance examination. These tests had been suspended eight years earlier when the chaos began. I passed and was accepted by Beijing University, where I majored in English. When I graduated, like all the graduates in China at the time, I was assigned a job by the government. I was told to report for work at the Chinese Secret Service because I was a single woman and had no parents—I, who had been called an enemy of China by the Red Guards!

Thanks to the changes and economic reforms sweeping

across China, I managed to have myself reassigned to the Foreign Affairs Department in Shanghai, where I was interpreter for Chinese officials who met with visiting dignitaries, government leaders, and politicians from English-speaking nations. Among them were American president Ronald Reagan; Canada's governor general, Jeanne Sauvé; and British prime minister Margaret Thatcher. In 1986 I was invited to a reception held by Queen Elizabeth II when she visited Shanghai. I shook hands with her and her husband as they greeted their guests on the royal yacht *Britannia*.

At York University I audited courses, which meant I attended lectures and wrote the assignments and tests but wouldn't be given academic credit because I couldn't afford the tuition fees. And after only a couple of weeks, I became aware that my scholarship, which I had considered a king's ransom, wouldn't even get me through the year. I had to find a way to bring in some extra money.

But there was a problem. I had never applied for a job in my life, and I didn't know how.

While I was growing up in China, before being sent away to the farm, I had never had a job, nor had anyone else my age. No students took jobs, whether they were in secondary school or university. Such a thing was unheard of. From the day we started school, our parents and teachers made it clear that our sole task was to learn and to score good marks so we could qualify for better high schools and for university. On top of that, in a country with a huge and fast-growing population, jobs were always in short supply. When our schooling was over, the government alone would decide each person's occupation and location of employment.

Irene and "Ding," the older couple with whom I was staying, became my job-search instructors. Puffing on his pipe, Ding showed me the part of the newspaper where job openings were listed and explained how to interpret the wording in the want ads, revealing a brand-new culture to me. As I slowly read through page after page of jobs waiting to be filled, my hopes soared. Surely there must be something for me among these hundreds of lines of small print.

But I was nervous about making inquiries by telephone. What was the protocol for this kind of phone call? Would a simple "hello" be enough? Or should I make polite small talk first? If so, what should I say? Should I ask, "Have you eaten yet?" as we do in China?

Day by day, as I pored over the job descriptions, my confidence leaked away. One minute I was unsure of what I was qualified to do in Canada, the next I became frustrated with myself for feeling this way. I reminded myself over and over that I was a professional interpreter and had two university degrees and was now a full-time student at York. What on earth was I worried about?

The first ad I answered asked for a "housekeeper." At Beijing University I had studied an English novel by Daphne du Maurier called *Rebecca*. One of the characters, Mrs. Danvers, was a housekeeper. I remembered her very well, an intimidating woman who carried a bundle of iron keys at her waist and had charge of the entire household, including servants. I talked it over with Irene and Ding, and we agreed that this housekeeping position didn't sound like the one described in the book. I screwed up my courage and made the call.

"Hello?" said a woman with a heavy accent of some kind. "Who's that?"

Of course, I also had an accent, so we had trouble understanding each other at first. After a few moments it became clear that the "housekeeper" duties this job entailed didn't even come close to Mrs. Danvers's responsibilities. The woman wanted a cleaning lady. But she wasn't at all certain she wanted me, even after I assured her that I had lots of experience and knew how to scrub, mop, and wash, all by hand. She started to quiz me, asking what cleaning products I would use for various tasks—detergents, stain removers, floor polish, tile cleansers—rattling off a bewildering list of brand names.

I knew none of them.

"How would you get the stains off a stove top?" she pressed on.

I rummaged through my imagination. At home, our two-ring gas burner didn't have a "top," and few apartments were equipped with the kind of kitchen that seemed to be the norm in every Toronto household. I mumbled something about scrubbing really hard.

"You have nice day," she said, and hung up.

I was speechless and depressed, overwhelmed by the revelation that I wasn't even qualified to be a cleaning woman in Canada. But I am a mother, I reminded myself the next day. There were lots of babysitters wanted. I had taken care of my daughter, who was still in China, waiting for me to bring her to Canada. Babies are the same the world over, aren't they?

"Do you have any experience with babies?" asked Patty, the next woman I called.

Her words were music to my ears. "Yes, I have a daughter. She's six now."

"That's great," she replied. "Did you breast-feed her?"

My jaw dropped. What kind of question was that? How else would I have fed my daughter? Was this a trick? A test? I felt the urge to tell her that when my daughter was a baby, I rode my bicycle across Shanghai every day for her noon feeding. Rain or shine, I pedalled from my office to my home, six days a week, for nine months. But I decided the best answer was the simplest one.

"Yes."

"That's wonderful."

Wonderful?

Patty went on to explain that she needed "in-home child care" for her six-month-old son when she was involved in a project. "When I work, I can't be disturbed," she said, without specifying what kind of work she did. She told me where she lived and invited me to an interview. I was thrilled to learn that her apartment was very close to York University, and, if I got the job, I could easily get there after my classes.

On Saturday, I took the streetcar and two subways to her neighbourhood, located her high-rise, then rode the elevator to the seventh floor. Patty answered my knock and let me into a bright and spacious apartment. She took my jacket, hung it in the closet, pointed to a closed door, and said in a hushed voice, "Alex is asleep. Let's go to the kitchen."

We sat down at the table next to a large window, and Patty offered me a cup of tea. She was a sandy-haired, slender woman in her mid-thirties. And she was a "freelance journalist." I knew what a journalist was, but I had no idea what *freelance* meant. I decided to ask her later, if I got the position. She worked at home, she went on, and my job would be to look after Alex: to feed him, change his diaper, and play with him.

"I need absolute silence when I write," Patty emphasized again. "Otherwise I can't concentrate."

We talked a bit more before she gave me details of Alex's feeding schedule. Then she got up and pulled open the refrigerator door.

"Let me show you," she said.

Inside, on the top shelf, stood two ranks of baby bottles, all full and tightly capped. The bottles in the left column were marked with blue labels, the ones on the right with green.

"The blue ones are baby formula. The green bottles contain breast milk," said Patty cheerfully, closing the fridge door. She pointed to a sheet of paper stuck on the door with a magnet in the shape of a smiling cat, and continued. "The feeding chart is here. All you need to do is heat the bottle in the microwave. Just follow the instructions."

My mind remained inside the fridge with the green-labelled bottles. Breast milk?

Hers?

What was breast milk doing in the fridge? And how did it get into the bottles? What was the point of putting it in jars when all she had to do was unbutton her blouse when Alex was hungry? I began to wonder what kind of strange journalist she was.

I struggled to keep up with her detailed instructions: Wash my hands before handling the bottles. Remove the cap before heating the bottle in the microwave. Use only sterile nipples. Test the temperature on the inside of my wrist before feeding. None of these complications would be necessary, I said to myself, if Patty kept her breast milk where it belonged.

"Now let's go into the nursery," Patty said, leading the way.

Alex was sleeping in a crib against one wall, his face turned away. He had light golden hair, and his tiny back rose and fell with each breath. I couldn't help thinking of my daughter when she was that age.

Beside the crib was an elaborate table with a belt across the top. Shelves below and above it were laden with jars, boxes, and stacks of brightly coloured, folded objects that I took to be baby napkins.

"The diapers are here," Patty said, confirming my suspicions. "Here are the ointment, the wipes, and the baby powder. Don't use the ointment unless Alex has a rash or a red bottom. The soiled diaper bin is over there, in the corner."

As she talked I picked up and unfolded a diaper. No wonder it looked so puffy—it was lined with paper! But how could it be washed? When I saw the bin Patty had mentioned, it dawned on me. Patty threw the used diapers away. I couldn't help remembering Granny Ningbo, who lived down the hall from my apartment in Shanghai and used to take care of my infant daughter during the day when I was working. Granny Ningbo hand-washed my baby's diapers in the building's courtyard as she chatted with neighbours. I saw in my mind little white flags, worn thin with constant use, fluttering on a clothesline in the wind and sun, and I recalled my own hands, raw and red from scrubbing my daughter's clothes on a washboard each morning before I left for work.

A few moments later, Patty left the room. She walked down the long hall and closed the door behind her.

I returned to the kitchen, opened the fridge, and stared at the bottles lined up shoulder to shoulder like little soldiers, wondering once again how Patty got her breast milk from its natural place to a glass container—and why she would want to do so in the first place. Shaking my head, I slipped the feeding schedule from under its cat magnet and studied it. The next feeding was in about a half-hour, formula this time. I replaced the list and removed a blue-labelled bottle from the fridge. Washing my hands, I unscrewed the cap and placed the bottle beside the microwave to be ready. Then I heard a muted cry from the nursery.

Alex was a beautiful and healthy boy. As I changed his wet diaper, he cooed and gurgled as if I were an old friend. His fair hair, blue eyes, and soft, white skin were a total contrast to any babies I had seen throughout my life—all of whom were black-haired and dark-eyed. Alex smelled of powder and cream and soap. He seemed to draw the tension out of me, and I began to relax a bit. I hoped this job would work out so that my money worries be over, and I knew I would enjoy being with Alex for a few hours each day.

I dressed Alex in a fresh one-piece outfit, dotted with blue and red balloons on a yellow background, thinking all the while how cleverly it was designed, with a zipper from the instep of one foot all the way to the neck. I strapped him into his reclining baby seat as Patty had shown me. I was convinced that Canada must have legions of brilliant and devoted engineers for babies.

I set Alex's seat on the kitchen table and heated the formula. He was hungry and quickly sucked the bottle dry. Holding him to my shoulder, I patted his back until I heard his satisfied burp. For a long while, I carried him around aimlessly, singing and talking to him. I tried to remember if I had ever held my daughter for so long when she was little. It seemed that I was always so busy, always in a hurry, and always with a long list of things to do as soon as I returned home: washing, cleaning, shopping, and cooking. I wished I had done things differently, and I wished, at that moment, that I had my daughter with me.

Held snugly against my ribs, Alex drifted off to sleep. I placed him gently in his crib, feeling a bit lost. Then I looked around for something else to do. There was no sign of Patty, no sound coming from the front of the apartment other than the occasional ringing of a phone. I noticed an overflowing laundry basket beside the changing table and began to fold the clothes.

I was almost finished when Patty appeared in the open doorway. She indicated silently that I should follow her into the kitchen. Closing the door of Alex's room, I joined her there.

"I'm through my work for today," she said, smiling. "You seem to get along with Alex very well, so, if you agree, I'd like to make this a permanent arrangement."

"You mean I got the job?"

"Yes."

"Thank you!" I could hardly contain my excitement.

"I just need to see your permit."

"My ... sure," I replied quickly, thinking she must mean my passport and visa, to make sure I was who I claimed to be. And who could blame her? If I were her, I would do the same, and not so lightly let a stranger look after my baby. I fetched my purse from the hall table. I was glad that I had brought all the documents with me: my passport, my visa, the letter of invitation from the university, and Irene and Ding's home address and phone number as my reference. Nevertheless, Patty's request caused a small current of uneasiness, reminding me of my years of constant anxiety in China under the scrutiny of authority figures such as police and party officials.

Back in the kitchen, I pulled my passport out of my purse and handed it to Patty. I stood before her as she turned the maroon-coloured booklet over in her hands, flipping through the pages. She looked up slowly, then frowned. My apprehension grew. Her silence worried me. Hands shaking, I quickly placed the letter of invitation from York University on the table in front of her. Instead, Patty fixed her eyes on me.

"None of these is a work permit," she said finally, with an edge in her voice. Her previously open, friendly face clouded with anger.

"A work—"

"You have to have one to take a job in Canada," she continued.

"But I—"

"Are you trying to get me in trouble? Do you know what could happen to me if I hired an illegal?"

"An illegal? Me?" I asked, my voice quavering.

Patty was accusing me of breaking the law. Would she call police? Would I be arrested and sent back to China in disgrace?

"Please," I pleaded, embarrassed by the tears streaming down my face. "I have never committed a crime in my life."

"Didn't you know you must have a work permit to take a job in Canada?"

"No, I ... Nobody told me about a permit. Please don't call the police. I'll leave right now," I added, snatching up my papers and stuffing them into my purse.

"Wait," Patty said.

I raised my eyes and looked at her. The anger had left her face, and she too appeared confused. "Don't cry," she said. "I'm sorry if I scared you. I didn't mean to ... I just ... Look, sit down."

I remained standing, afraid to trust her and eager to get out of her sight. This woman who had seemed so open and friendly was so agitated, she couldn't finish her own sentence.

"I have to go," I said again, making for the door.

"Wait. Please," Patty called out. "Let me at least pay you for your time."

As I trudged along the deserted street, Patty's words kept playing in my mind. I couldn't comprehend the kind of trouble Patty might have faced if she had hired me to look after her little boy, but I was used to tight government controls, some of them illogical or foolish. Yet, until then, it had never occurred to me that in some parts of the world, a person's willingness to work would be challenged and even punished under the law. Maybe Canada and China weren't as radically different as I had imagined. What a world we live in, I thought. Long ago, when I was only a teen, I was forced to leave home and to endure backbreaking labour in order to survive. Now I had come to Canada and was willing to take any job to fulfill my dreams. But a piece of paper stood in my way. What was I going to do? Would I give up so easily?

"Hello," I said. "I'm calling about the babysitting job you posted in the paper. I wonder if it's still available."

"Yes, it is," a man's voice replied. "Are you interested?"

"Yes, I am," I replied, realizing I sounded more confident and calmer than I felt. "But I would like you to know before we go any further that I don't have a work permit."

"Oh, that. Don't worry about the permit. My parents were immigrants." He paused for a second. "How about coming to the house on Saturday, so we can talk about it? Say, two o'clock?"

"Thank you," I said. "I'll be there."

THE CONTRIBUTORS

 SVETLANA CHMAKOVA was born and raised in Russia and moved to Canada with her family when she was almost sixteen years old. After high school, she earned a three-year diploma in classical animation from Sheridan College and spent several years as a freelance illustrator/animator. Svetlana's comics career suddenly took off with the publication of her first full-length manga series, *Dramacon*, which became a fan favourite as well as critically acclaimed. Svetlana has also worked on a monthly one-page manga for *CosmoGirl!* magazine for two years and recently on art-directing a fifty-two-episode animated show for Teletoon.

Currently Svetlana is working on her next manga series, *Nightschool*, an urban fantasy for young adults set in a school for witches, vampires, and werewolves.

Svetlana lives in Ontario with her family and sometimes updates her website: www.svetlania.com.

RACHNA GILMORE is a bestselling, Governor General's Award–winning author of numerous children's books, including picture books, such as the popular Gita series; early- and middle-grade novels, such as *Mina's Spring of Colors*; and young adult novels, such as *A Group of One* and *The Sower of Tales*. Rachna's books have been translated into several languages, and she gives presentations in schools, libraries, and conferences across Canada as well as internationally. Her latest releases include the novel *The Trouble with Dilly* and the picture book *Catching Time*. Born in India, Rachna has lived in London, England, and Prince Edward Island, and now calls Ottawa home.

LINDA GRANFIELD has written nearly thirty information books for young readers and adults. Her award-winning titles include *In Flanders Fields: The Story of the Poem by John McCrae* (called "the red book at Remembrance Day" by Canadian students). Her history books, primarily about the First and Second World Wars, were written to help readers connect with the veterans in their families and communities. She has also worked on television and radio, and contributed to an international documentary film.

RICHARDO KEENS-DOUGLAS was born in Grenada. His career leaps many disciplines: actor, writer, director, and storyteller. It is also a career of many firsts, including the first black host to have his own hour-long network show, *Cloud 9* on CBC.9, as well as the first host of the

Caribbean version of the hit show *Who Wants to Be a Millionaire*. As an actor, Richardo has had numerous roles in film and television and countless appearances onstage. Richardo has written six plays, including *The Nutmeg Princess*, which won the 1999 Dora Mavor Moore Award for Outstanding Musical. In 2003, he was inducted into the Caribbean Hall of Fame for Excellence in Theatre. Richardo has also written ten children's books, including *Tales from the Island of Spice*, which won the Golden Oak Award in 2005. Finally, Richardo is an in-demand motivational speaker and storyteller who has delighted audiences throughout North America and the Caribbean.

 ALICE KUIPERS was born in London, England. She moved to Saskatoon in 2003, where she lives with her partner and their baby. Her award-winning first novel, *Life on the Refrigerator Door*, has been published in twenty-eight countries, all of which she'd like to visit one day because she loves to travel. Her second novel, *The Worst Thing She Ever Did*, is coming out in 2010. When she's not writing, she teaches Pilates and attempts to garden, having no idea about flowers, planting, or how to cope with temperatures that range from minus forty to plus thirty-five.

 RACHEL MANLEY was born in Cornwall, England, grew up in Jamaica, and now lives in Toronto. She is the author of *Drumblair: Memories of a Jamaican Childhood*, which won the Governor General's Literary Award for Nonfiction in 1997, and *Slipstream: A Daughter Remembers*, a memoir of her father, Michael Manley, former prime minister of Jamaica. She has published three books of poetry and edited

Edna Manley: The Diaries, a collection of her grandmother's journals.

The name Boonaa, in Afan Oromo, means "proud," and BOONAA MOHAMMED's work has made a growing audience very proud. Child of refugee parents from Oromia, a part of Ethiopia still under a colonial regime, Boonaa learned about the power of words at a young age. His parents left the country because their outspoken criticisms of the current government put themselves and their children's lives at risk. As a child, Boonaa faced many issues being a first-generation Canadian; the cultural gap between his parents and their new country forced him to navigate much of his youth alone. Known in arts circles across Canada, Boonaa first made a name for himself on the slam-poetry circuit by winning most major competitions in Toronto; he was crowned the 2007 CBC Poetry Face-Off "Best New Artist." Currently finishing up a degree in radio and television broadcasting at Ryerson University, Boonaa has crossed over into the world of theatre, with his play entitled *Purple Don't Cry* set for production in the near future.

MAHTAB NARSIMHAN, a native of Mumbai, plays with acronyms during the day and with words at night, when she does all her writing. She has always been fascinated by Indian mythology and adventure. This passion came together with the unique cultural and spiritual energies of her homeland in her debut novel, *The Third Eye*, winner of the Silver Birch Fiction Award in 2009. A sequel, *The Silver Anklet*, was published in 2009. Mahtab lives in Toronto with her husband, Rahul, and her son, Aftab.

DIMITRI NASRALLAH was born in Lebanon in 1977 and arrived in Canada in 1988. He is the author of the 2005 novel *Blackbodying*, which won the Quebec Writers' Federation McAuslan First Book Award and was a finalist for the Grand Prix du livre de Montréal. His short fiction won the 2006 CBC Quebec Writing Competition. His writing has appeared in *The Globe and Mail*, *Exclaim!*, Toronto's *Eye Weekly*, the Montreal *Gazette*, the *Montreal Review of Books*, *Maisonneuve*, and numerous other publications. He is currently at work on a second novel.

MARINA NEMAT was born in 1965 in Tehran, Iran. After the Islamic Revolution of 1979, she was arrested at the age of sixteen and spent more than two years in Evin, a political prison in Tehran, where she was tortured and came very close to being executed. She came to Canada in 1991 and has called it home ever since. In 2005 she was a finalist in the creative nonfiction category of the CBC Literary Awards, and in 2006, she produced a documentary named *Walls Like Snakes* for CBC Radio. Her memoir of her life in Iran, *Prisoner of Tehran*, published by Penguin Canada in April 2007, has been published in twenty-three other countries and is an international bestseller. *Maclean's* magazine calls it "one of the finest (memoirs) ever written by a Canadian." *Prisoner of Tehran* has been shortlisted for many literary awards, including the YoungMinds Book Award in the United Kingdom and the Borders Original Voices Award in the United States. On

December 15, 2007, Marina received the inaugural Human Dignity Prize from the European Parliament, and in October 2008, she received the prestigious Grinzane Prize in Italy. She is now an Aurea Fellow at the University of Toronto's Massey College, where she is working on her new book.

RICHARD POPLAK is the author of the acclaimed *Ja, No, Man: Growing Up White in Apartheid-Era South Africa* and *The Sheikh's Batmobile: In Pursuit of American Pop Culture in the Muslim World*. He has written for, among other publications, the *Walrus*, *This Magazine*, *Toronto Life*, and *The Globe and Mail* and has directed numerous short films, music videos, and commercials. He lives in Toronto.

RUI UMEZAWA returned to wrestling after moving to Edmonton in 1975 and is today an avid martial artist. He is the author of three books, including the novel *The Truth About Death and Dying*, which was nominated for the Commonwealth Writers Prize, Best First Book in 2003. He now lives in Toronto with his wife and three children and is working on his next novel.

EVA WISEMAN writes historical fiction for young adults. Her books include *Puppet*, *My Canary Yellow Star*, *No One Must Know*, *A Place Not Home*, and *Kanada*, which won the Geoffrey Bilson Award for Historical Fiction for Young People and was a finalist for the Governor General's Literary Awards. Eva's books have been also published in the United States and Europe.

Eva immigrated to Canada as a young girl during the Hungarian Revolution in 1956. She never forgot her roots, and her experiences as an immigrant are the basis of several of her novels.

Eva lives in Winnipeg with her husband and father. She has two grown children and six young grandchildren.

 TING-XING YE, born in Shanghai in 1952, was an English interpreter for the Chinese government before leaving China in 1987. Her memoir, *A Leaf in the Bitter Wind*, has been published in nine countries. She is also the author of *Throwaway Daughter* and the award-winning *White Lily*. She lives in Orillia, Ontario.

ACKNOWLEDGMENTS

One of the best things about being a writer is that you get to acknowledge everyone who was instrumental in the birth of your book and render their names to eternity, or at least for the length of the print run. My immortals for this project are my family, my first readers, my first cheerleaders, Ken, Sasha, and Nikki Toten; and my tireless writing "Goup," Susan Adach, Ann Goldring, Nancy Hartry, and Loris Lesynski. I am deeply grateful to Leona Trainer, Marie Campbell, and David Bennett of Transatlantic Literary Agency (TLA), who each held this project aloft when it needed holding, as did Barbara Berson. It was an absolute joy working with my partner in crime, editor Jennifer Notman, and I am grateful for Marcia Gallego's elegant copy edit. Finally, I salute each of the contributing writers. They bared their souls and their stories and entrusted them to me. It was an honour. Thank you all.

COPYRIGHT
ACKNOWLEDGMENTS